Distant Mountains

To my friend, Anthony, who appreciates the beauty below from the view above! Maybe you'll even experience some of these views first hand! Happy Birthday!

Your friend — Tammy

Distant Mountains

ENCOUNTERS WITH THE WORLD'S GREATEST MOUNTAINS

PHOTOGRAPHY BY JOHN CLEARE

DISCOVERY CHANNEL BOOKS

RANDOM HOUSE, INC.

*To my climbing companions over the years,
without whose company, friendship and
patience the photographs in this book
would never have been taken.*

Distant Mountains
Photography by John Cleare

Copyright © 1998 Duncan Baird Publishers
Copyright of photographs © 1998 John Cleare
Commissioned illustrations, maps, and studio photography copyright © 1998 Duncan Baird Publishers
Copyright of Introduction, pp.8–9, and Factfiles © John Cleare

For copyright of individual articles, see page 176, which is to be regarded as an extension of this copyright page.

All rights reserved under International and Pan-American Copyright Conventions.
Published in the United States by Random House Inc., New York
in association with Discovery Channel Publishing

Created and designed by
Duncan Baird Publishers Ltd, London

Designer: Gabriella Le Grazie
Managing editor: Judy Dean
Commissioning consultant: Audrey Salkeld
Editor: Zoë Ross
Studio photography: David Murray
Commissioned artwork and maps: Robert Nelmes
Calligraphy: Susanne Haines

A Cataloging-in-Publication data listing for this book is available from the Library of Congress.

ISBN: 0-679-46255-4

Random House Website
www.randomhouse.com

Discovery Communications, Inc., produces high-quality non-fiction television programming, interactive media,
books, films, and consumer products. Discovery Networks, a division of Discovery Communications, Inc.,
operates and manages Discovery Channel, TLC (The Learning Channel), Animal Planet, and Travel Channel.
Visit our website at http://www.discovery.com/

Typeset in 10pt Sabon
Color reproduction by Colourscan, Singapore
Printed in Italy

1 3 5 7 9 10 8 6 4 2

PUBLISHER'S NOTE
The captions in this book are by John Cleare.
In all the pieces both imperial (feet etc.) and metric units are given for altitudes and other dimensions. This
has required the adjustment of the authors' original text in some cases. "The Light of Other Days" (Canadian
Rockies; pp.56–69) is exceptional in putting metric before imperial units. The exception was made for the sake
of consistency with a passage in which David Harris refers specifically to the question of measurement.

Contents

Introduction

The first mountain I remember was Snowdon. My grandmother pointed out its distant blue shape and I recall the smoke from the invisible train as it puffed towards the summit. My granny had climbed Snowdon on her honeymoon before the railway came and now I desperately wanted to reach the top myself. But I rather resented that train: surely that was no way to climb a mountain?

I was just four at the time and ever afterwards I was aware of mountains, taking it for granted that one day, when I was old enough, I would climb not only Snowdon but other mountains too. Meanwhile there were trees to climb, a serious activity that was much more fun than playing ball games. Later, at school, I was privileged to use the personal mountain library of one of the masters. Thus I had already imbibed Winthrop Young and Kirkus and studied the photographs of Abrahams and Smythe when I eventually tied on the rope and set off up my very first mountain, Tryfan in Snowdonia, at the age of thirteen. I knew then that mountains were to play an important part in my life.

Early on I learnt that technical climbing, although the activity that most engrossed an adventurous youth, is merely one part of the art of mountaineering – the art of moving safely in steep and potentially hazardous mountainous terrain. The complete mountaineer must be adept on steep rock, snow and ice and be an expert hill-walker, a proficient navigator and a competent off-piste skier. He – or she – should also be a skilled back-packer, camper and survivor, besides having a working knowledge of wilderness medicine, meteorology, geology, glaciology, natural history – and more.

Since that scramble on Tryfan I've enjoyed some of the hardest rock-climbs and most challenging alpine ascents of the day; I've climbed my fill of new routes and several virgin summits. But expeditions among the Greater Ranges, formal and well-organised attempts to climb a specific mountain, even when successful, have always left something to be desired. My greatest delight has been to travel light with an old friend among new mountains with no set objectives. We have climbed mountains because they looked enticing not because they were famous, we have crossed passes to see what was on the other side, we have drawn our own maps because the official ones were wrong. We were proving nothing, writing no glowing reports. The ethos was pure – that of Tilman and Shipton – and the style unfortunately against the regulations in many places today.

But mountains are all things to all men; there are no rules, no agendas. We can each find among them that which we seek, be it inspiration, achievement, healthy exercise or escape – none or all of these things. John Ruskin put it pretty succinctly:

"... these threatening ranges of dark mountains ... are in reality sources of life and happiness far fuller and more beneficent than the bright fruitfulness of the plain."

John Cleare

ABOUT THE PHOTOGRAPHS, FACTFILES AND MAPS

I delight in taking photographs. There is, nevertheless, a professional motive behind every image I shoot and the pictures in this book have been taken on various assignments or for my library over a number of years. Mountain photography is at once a simple yet difficult task: simple because usually subjects abound and inspiration comes easily; difficult because of the practical constraints imposed by the mountains themselves.

Much as I regret not carrying a camera on the best of my early climbs, doing so might well have jeopardised both success and safety. It requires extraordinary dedication to change film when fighting for survival in a blizzard. And one tends to be parsimonious with pictures when carrying three weeks supply of film stock – together with everything else – on one's back.

The mountain photographer, to cope adequately, must carry a certain minimum of equipment and typically I need to carry some 12 lbs (5.5kg) more than my companions. I use 35mm Nikons – the supreme go-anywhere professional camera – or occasionally in this book a Fuji 6x17 panoramic camera. The latter, awkward to carry and difficult to use in rugged conditions, produces unusual and exciting images of a shape unfortunately limited in its commercial application. The prolific mountain photographer works hard for his pictures.

Just as mountain photography is essentially extreme landscape photography, so mountain writing is an extreme form of travel literature. In both disciplines the context is important and, to misquote a well-used aphorism, a map is worth a thousand words. Space has limited our Factfiles to far less than a thousand words and our basic but succinct maps to the bare minimum necessary to show the context of the photographs and the articles. Most mountaineers – most travellers – enjoy researching their next expedition and there are facts enough here to assist enthused readers to home in on detailed maps and guide books.

Photographing mountains is a gratifying business and I've greatly enjoyed working through my files to select the pictures for this book. Through them I've re-lived great days, rekindled powerful emotions and evoked memories long forgotten. Photography, of all art forms, best possesses this special property and my profession is to use it to communicate something of those feelings to others. Aided by erudite writers whose work I greatly respect, I hope that in this book I have succeeded in that task.

John Cleare

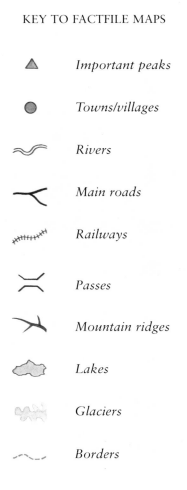

KEY TO FACTFILE MAPS

▲   *Important peaks*

●   *Towns/villages*

〜   *Rivers*

✕   *Main roads*

✕   *Railways*

✕   *Passes*

✕   *Mountain ridges*

☁   *Lakes*

  Glaciers

〜   *Borders*

Mohammed's Bridge

The Pyrenees

NICHOLAS CRANE

*"Dropping away in front of me was a desert of bare rock speckled with
fragments of old glacier and small lakes. Brown sierras shimmered in the
distance. There was no sign of vegetation or of paths. I set the compass,
then slithered down the scree. Behind me, the Brèche receded until it
was a small window set in the wall between France and Spain.
So close to teeming Gavarnie, I could hardly believe
I'd stepped into such a bleak wilderness."*

RIGHT: *We look west from Hourquette d'Alans over the head of the Gavarnie valley towards Vignemale – on the skyline right of centre. The Pouey Aspé valley is clearly seen leading up to the Port de Boucharo saddle at left of centre, while the Brèche de Roland slashes the skyline, far left.*

RIGHT: *We look west from Hourquette d'Alans over the head of the Gavarnie valley towards Vignemale – on the skyline right of centre. The Pouey Aspé valley is clearly seen leading up to the Port de Boucharo saddle at left of centre, while the Brèche de Roland slashes the skyline, far left.*

BELOW: *This is the Port de Boucharo – perhaps one of the easiest passes in the High Pyrenees. The view looks down into Spain.*

By the fourth day in Gavarnie my sleeping-bag was dry and the clouds had moved on. With a *pan de paysan* jammed in the top of my rucksack, I walked up to the church. As I sat in the cool shadows a man with heavy spectacles emerged from a door beside the altar and sat at the organ. He let his fingers wander to and fro across the keys, picking up bars from Satie to Schubert while sunlight played beyond the open door on the geraniums and the graves and the birds chirruped a chorus. In this exquisite moment it occured to me that beauty cannot be sought; one simply has to put oneself in the way of its whims, and wait.

The path climbed the open slopes of the Pouey Aspé valley. Parts remained of a laid stone surface, with foot-smoothed bedrock and an old embankment. Back when pilgrimages were made on foot, this was one of the converging branches of the *Chemin de St Jacques* – pilgrims who had included Lourdes on their journey to Santiago walked up the Pouey Aspé and through the 7,448-ft (2,270-metre) Port de Boucharo to Spain. In mist or snow or rain wearing a woollen cloak this would have been a terrifying hurdle, with every chance of missing the turn in the path at the foot of the Glacier du Taillon. Here I left the pilgrim's route and scrambled over the rocks to the Refuge des Sarradets, set impossibly on cliffs. The building looked as if it had fallen from the sky and lodged on a ledge.

The ridge above Sarradets was wafer-thin, eaten away from both sides by the freeze and thaw of ice. Above the hut the skyline was cut by the deep slot of the Brèche de Roland, sliced according to folklore by the dying Frank as he tried to prevent his sword, Durendal, falling into the hands of the Basques – a feat needing a long arm (or a telescopic prosthesis) since Roland was 62 miles (100 kilometres) away at Roncesvalles at the time. One of the earliest trippers (who now come along a level path from the road up to the Port de Boucharo) to visit the Brèche was the widow of the assassinated second son of King Charles X, the

Duchesse de Berry, who was carried up in 1822, in a chair. Henry Russell nearly lost his life here after being trapped for twelve hours by a storm. I stepped through the Brèche, into another land.

Dropping away in front of me was a desert of bare rock speckled with fragments of old glacier and small lakes. Brown sierras shimmered in the distance. There was no sign of vegetation or of paths. I set the compass, then slithered down the scree. Behind me, the Brèche receded until it was a small window set in the wall between France and Spain. So close to teeming Gavarnie, I could hardly believe I'd stepped into such a bleak wilderness. Three stone-coloured animals, *rebecos*, or perhaps the rare Pyrenean ibex, appeared in the distance. *Capra pyrenaica pyrenaica* – *bucardo* to the Spanish and *bouquetin* to the French – was decimated by the hunting guns of Sir Henry Halford, the crackshot Victorian author of *Art of Shooting with a Rifle*, and Sir Victor Brooke. The animals walked slowly over the rocks and disappeared beyond Pico Blanco.

A steep band of névé – the little Glacier de la Brèche – leads up to the imposing cleft of the Brèche de Roland on the French side. The far side is, as Nicholas Crane says, a very different landscape. Dry and desert-like, it is a parched land of far horizons.

Ian Howell pauses on the Col des Sarradets at the foot of the Taillon glacier, en route to the Refuge des Sarradets – here, seen on the right. He looks eastwards over the void of the Gavarnie Cirque to the convoluted strata of Pic du Marboré.

The compass led me to the Collado Blanco, a high saddle between 10,315-ft (3,144-metre) Taillon and Pico Blanco, and from here I picked my way down the loose gully on the west side of the *collado*, towards the feature marked on my dubious Spanish map as Aguas Tuertas, the One-eyed Lake. This would, I thought, make a pleasant bivouac site. But the gully ran out above a flat-bottomed bowl of grass. The lake had gone; evaporated, or drained away through some geological plughole.

The day was drawing in. I'd seldom felt so isolated: the enormous, whispering plateau was walled in to the north by Gavarnie's great ridge of rock, and cut off to the south by the unseen chasm of Ordesa. I measured isolation on a sliding scale of human decomposition, based on the amount of time my body would lie before being discovered by a passerby. Up here, we were unquestionably thinking in terms of skeleton.

Intermittent cairns led along the side of a cleft which split Pico Salarons from Mondarruego – the twin peaks dominating the northern end of the Ordesa canyon – to the brink of a cliff. Leaving my rucksack on a rock, I

climbed down the cliff, on to a sloping, grassy pediment strewn with debris from the cliffs above. I was probably on the Faja Luenga – one of the ledges which separated the strata of the canyon walls. Below me was another brink. I leaned over the edge. Some 3,000 feet (1,000 metres) down, already deep in dusk, was the floor of the Ordesa canyon.

Set back a few feet from the brink were two gigantic rocks, one of them split in two and clenching, like a nutcracker, a boulder. Beneath the rocks was a fin of limestone just high enough to protect my prone body from the wind. It would make a fine bivouac site. I fetched my rucksack and, with another thirty minutes of light left, set out to explore the ledge.

My bivouac site was in a "bay" set between two headlands in the wall of the canyon. I followed the ledge west and was surprised to find a path which crept round beneath the cliffs of Mondarruego to the headland marked on my map as El Retablo – The Altar. The thin prow of rock jutted into the canyon, topped by a knoll of grass. I stood in the last of the sun, watching the fire of the day burn out over the western sierras, then returned to the nutcracker rock, where I lit a small fire from dead roots I'd collected on the ledge and heated a mugful of water for soup. Above the cliffs, satellites and shooting stars scored the blackboard night.

I woke once, snapped from sleep by the sound of a gunshot. Its echoes mingled with crashes and then a long rattle of stones, as a piece of cooling cliff prised itself away from warmth-retaining bedrock.

At first light I followed the Faja Luenga eastwards to the headland facing El Retablo and lay in the rising sun warming my bones beside a dwarf pine, as alone and magnificently fragile as a bonsai, balanced on a toy lawn surrounded on three sides by emptiness. In daylight, Ordesa revealed itself as a smaller Grand Canyon, with layered cliffs facing with stomach-churning verticality into the shadowed abyss.

After some false starts I found the first of the *clavijas* – ladders of metal pegs – leading down the cliff. Below the cliff, the angle eased and a path slithered down to the tree-line, then cut to and fro through the thickening layers of vegetation clinging to the canyon wall. Through box and oak and pine, the air warmed; beech and fir began to appear, and then a thickening of the undercover as ferns and rhododendrons breathed the rising humid air. By the time I stepped from the forest into the spacious birches by the shingle banks of the Río Araza, my shirt was heavy with sweat.

TOP: *This is the strange limestone dome of El Descargador flaunting its exposed strata for all to see on the Spanish flanks below the Brèche de Roland.*

BOTTOM: *Bivouacking is the best way to experience the many moods of the mountains. Ian Howell stirs the evening brew on a grassy ledge below Monte Perdido. Finding water was difficult on these limestone hillsides.*

A 1,970-foot (600-metre) climb up the facing wall of the canyon lifted me to the Faja de Pelay. The most trodden of Ordesa's ledge-paths followed the 6,234-foot (1,900-metre) contour along a second band of strata, for about 5 miles (8 kilometres), towards the canyon head. I slept beside the path and continued next morning along this linear belvedere, pausing to lie among the rocks watching a flock of *rebecos* picking their way delicately across a scree. Finally the line of strata on the canyon walls converged with the rising slope of canyon floor, then met at the canyon head where a fan-shaped waterfall, the Cola de Caballo – Horse's Tail – fell to a level meadow divided by the infant Araza. Ahead, the horizon was blocked by the highest limestone massif in Europe: Monte Perdido.

A path climbed to the Refugio de Goriz and then up to a broad pass at 7,641 feet (2,329 metres), where I turned to the north over the flanks of Monte Perdido on a route which had been described to me in the refuge as *peligroso* and which my guidebook warned was "awful" and "not recommended". The attraction of this route was that it skirted the head of the Ordesa's little sister, Añisclo.

The path (understandably, as I was about to discover) was little used. Having reached about 8,200 feet (2,500 metres) on the Pico de Añisclo (the southern buttress of Monte Perdido), the route inched nervously over screes that threatened to slide over cliffs, then scaled and descended a series of sloping slabs lubricated by grit and water. It was midday and on the south-facing slope of Monte Perdido all I could see of Añisclo was a black jagged rent, directly beneath my boots. It was as if someone had torn a gâteau in half, clumsily. Beyond the gorge rolled the hazed waves of dusty sierras, sailed by cloud-ships.

We descended the ice-hung northern flank of the Cuello del Cilindro – the slot in the skyline just right of Monte Perdido (seen in the background) – into a strange hanging valley between Perdido and the frontier crest. Here we crossed these gravelly flats to the cool, green Lago de Marboré.

I emerged on Collado de Añisclo, an airy 3,280-foot (1,000-metre) blade falling to Añisclo on one side and to the smooth, 12-kilometre glaciated groove of Pineta on the other, a pine-covered perfect U, framed by the parallel precipices of the Sierra de las Tucas and the Sierra de Espierba.

Descents from the heights were always weighted with small forebodings. Life down below was a lot more complicated. The plummet into Pineta was also physically painful; for over 3,900 feet (1,200 metres) inconceivably balanced rock and scree fell so steeply that, by the time I stepped down to the banks of the Cinca, daylight was finished and so were my knees.

*   *   *

Two men picked their way towards me, a Tyrolese guide leading his German client; one grimly looking, the other looking grim. I had seen their Porsche arrive at the road-head in the Esera valley the previous evening. The client, a banker from Frankfurt, was making a last stand against middle age.

This is Monte Perdido, a fine mountain and third highest in the Pyrenees. We are on the final slopes below the Cuello del Cilindro, high above Pequeno Lago Helado – the "Tiny Frozen Tarn". The regular route up Perdido ascends the wide hollow above the lake while the left skyline rising from the Cuello provides a sporting ridge climb.

It was on this mountain massif in 1897 that Stephen Spender's father, Harold, had a celebrated falling-out with his guide. The incident is related with polite ire in Spender's book *Through the High Pyrenees* and it neatly illustrates the pitfalls of allowing self-reliance to be subjugated by the will of the "local expert". Spender and his party – H. Llewellyn Smith, their French guide, Pierre Pujo, and a local man, "Chico" ("Boy"), whom they'd employed as a porter – were standing on the foot of Pico Forcanada, an elegant double-spike to the east of Pico de Aneto, piling their unnecessary baggage on the Collado Alfred so that they could climb unencumbered to the summit. An argument ensued about the rope. Pujo, the guide, wanted to leave it behind, stating that ropes were used for crossing snow, not rocks. This was countered by his clients' insistence that this was not the case in Switzerland, where ropes were habitually used for rock-climbs.

"Never in the Pyrenees!" ruled the French guide. They left the rope at the col.

"After all," conceded Spender, with fatalistic prescience, "he knew the country better than we did."

The group set off up Pico Forcanada, following an increasingly sheer line which terminated in an overhanging cave, at which point Pujo announced that he was leading them up a new route. Pujo then unlaced his boots, handed them to Chico, and continued up the rock in his socks. Following his example, Spender and Smith also took off their boots and handed them to Chico, who strung them together and draped them over his shoulders like a necklace. In climbing the pitch, Pujo found himself stuck and had to be hauled up "hot and swearing" by Spender, a sight which so traumatized Chico that he refused to follow.

The three climbers now found themselves with no boots or rope at the top of a pitch which they could not climb down. "I know not how this would have ended," records Spender, "if I had not suddenly bethought me of a woollen muffler ..." Tying the scarf to the end of Pujo's red Pyrenean waistband, the men lowered their improvised rope to Chico, who tied the six boots to the end.

They reached the top of Forcanada, but on returning hungry and tired to the col discovered that the hapless Chico had bolted for the valley with all of their food and equipment. On the long, hungry descent, the exhausted Spender consoled himself by reciting Virgil: "*O passi graviora* ... O ye who have suffered greater woes."

Route-finding on the descent northwards from the Cuello del Cilindro is not easy. Steep slopes of ice and névé lead to a confusing sequence of rocky ledges and short walls. The cairns suggest someone has been here before! Ian Howell looks out towards Pic Blanc on the frontier above the head of the Valle de Pineta.

Above me, the Frankfurter and his leader had disappeared into the Portillón Superior, a notch in the ridge which drops to the tongue of Aneto's glacier. When I caught them up, they were moving slowly, roped together, through blasts of spindrift. New snow lay ankle-deep on the old glacier ice. They were dressed for the Antarctic, in glossy over-trousers and anoraks, mitts and crampons. I was wearing my spare pair of socks on my hands, my torn cotton trousers and jacket and worn-out walking boots. While my two companions were wearing climbing helmets, I had my trilby lashed to my head with the hood of my jacket. The guide, a terse character, understandably viewed my presence as a threat to his client's wellbeing. The banker, suffering on the steep, deep snow, was lost in personal oblivion.

Above us, clouds tore across Aneto. The guide picked a good line to the head of the glacier at Collado de Coronas. From here, the route led up rocks awash

This is the view from the Cuello del Cilindro eastwards along the Spanish side of the Pyrenean crest. Pico de Posets, second highest of the Pyrenean summits, stands on the horizon to the right of centre, with Pico de Aneto unseen behind it.

with powder-snow towards a summit obliterated by spindrift.

The top of Pico de Aneto was defended by the Pont de Mahomet, a tottering bridge of rocks with immense drops on both sides. On the snow hummock at the lower end of Pont de Mahomet the guide was coiling the rope ready to lead out across the rocks and shouting instructions into the German's ear. They were plastered with snow. It took the guide fifteen minutes to cajole the banker across the iced rocks while the gale buffeted his trembling legs. Through the flying snow, the two walked the few steps from the far end of the Pont de Mahomet, up to the cross on the summit of the mountain.

Watching their success through the spindrift, I realized that I couldn't bridge the gap alone. To negotiate the iced holds I needed the security of the rope. "A barrier shall divide the blessed from the damned," says the Koran, "and on the Heights there shall stand men who will know each of them by his look."

The guide didn't throw me the end of the rope. And I was not about to ask for it. I turned around and descended to La Renclusa.

The aptly named El Cilindro towers over Pequeno Lago Helado in the early morning sunshine. The route to the Cuello (literally meaning "the neck") – the saddle between El Cilindro and Monte Perdido – lies up the steep slabs left of the shadow.

THE PYRENEES – FACTFILE

BACKGROUND

Forming the border between Spain and France, the long narrow chain of the Pyrenees is essentially a single crest of sharp peaks rising high above surrounding foothills, quite extensive on the southern side. Only three summits reach 11,000ft (3,350m) but more than 50 top 10,000ft (3,050m) and there are several small glaciers. While granite forms several massifs, much of the range is limestone with complex topography, characteristic cliff-girt amphitheatres, high waterfalls and a major system of caves, potholes and underground watercourses. The range has always been a cultural and ethnic frontier. The development of serious mountaineering reflected that in the Alps although most of the summits were reached rather earlier, typically by French or Spanish worthies guided by local hunters.

ACCESS

Although parts of the Pyrenees are still remote and unfrequented, the mountain range forms an ever-popular vacation destination and, as elsewhere in Europe, hiking and climbing are unregulated. There are numerous village resorts, particularly on the French side where Lourdes, in the foothills 25 miles (40km) from Gavarnie, is a famous pilgrim centre.

Thanks to geography, access to the Spanish flank is not as easy, but there are several well-known ski resorts on either side of the frontier.

The range boasts more than 60 climbing huts and refuges, owned by French and Spanish alpine clubs, as well as the various national park authorities. Both flanks of the area described in Nicholas Crane's piece lie within national parks.

HIKING AND CLIMBING

A network of paths and trails covers the area described, many of them linking more than a dozen huts and refuges. Routes are diverse enough to suit those of varying ability: some are easy, while others are steep and rugged, and no great mountaineering prowess is necessary

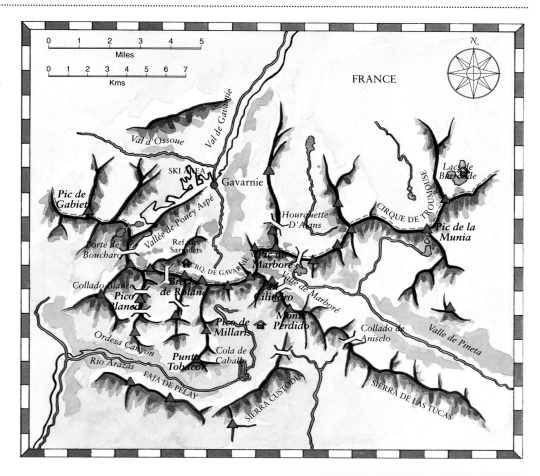

to ascend the straightforward routes which reach virtually every Pyrenean summit. The range is a paradise for serious scramblers – especially when combined with a back-packing expedition. Nevertheless, excellent rock climbing of all grades abounds on both the ridges and the walls of the craggy summits, as well as on the great cliffs such as those of the Ordesa Canyon and the 5,000-foot (1,500-m) Gavarnie Cirque.

Several classic ice routes date back as far as the 1880s, while the many waterfalls provide modern winter ice climbs of the highest standards. The Pico d'Aneto described in the article is the highest Pyrenean peak. First climbed in 1842, it rises from the granite Maladetta massif, a spur of the main crest some 27 miles (43km) east of Monte Perdido and entirely in Spain.

Pico de Aneto	*11,168ft / 3,404m*
Pico de Posets	*11,073ft / 3,375m*
Monte Perdido	*11,007ft / 3,355m*
El Cilindro	*10,919ft / 3,328m*
Pic du Marboré	*10,656ft / 3,248m*
Taillon	*10,315ft / 3,144m*
Pic de la Munia	*10,279ft / 3,133m*
Pico Blanco	*9,528ft / 2,904m*
Brèche de Roland	*9,199ft / 2,804m*
Punta Tobacor	*9,121ft / 2,780m*
Pic de Gabiet	*8,911ft / 2,716m*
Pico de Millaris	*8,609ft / 2,624m*
Refuge des Sarradets	*8,488ft / 2,587m*
Hourquette D'Alans	*7,972ft / 2,430m*
Porte de Boucharo	*7,448ft / 2,270m*
Gavarnie (village)	*4,495ft / 1,370m*

The Roof of the Alps

The Western Alps

W. M. CONWAY

*"Few ascents in the Alps are simpler than that of the Jungfrau
from the south for people who understand mountains.
There is none better worth making."*

MONT BLANC

By one o'clock the guides were stirring. A few minutes after two we were on our way. It took but a short quarter-of-an-hour to follow the steps made by Carrel in the evening, which the frost had turned into a staircase as of rock. Thus we emerged upon an easy snow-slope, whilst the moon, already in its last quarter, hung on the crest of the Rocher du Mont Blanc. For some distance above us the glacier was cut across by walls of ice with slopes of avalanche debris between, up which we wound to turn obstacles as they came. Step-cutting was almost continuously required, but the slopes were not steep and small chips sufficed. The dim light of future day soon rendered our lanterns useless. Greys and faint purples began to overspread the distant view; then dawn swept her rosy wing over all and the golden day appeared, full armed, on the margin of the east.

As the slopes became steeper and step-cutting more laborious and slow, there was time to look about and note the value of the regular pyramid of Mont Favre, standing out before the white sweeps and scoops of more distant mountains. But the eye seldom wandered so far afield; close at hand were objects of fascinating beauty. We were passing between cavernous crevasses, and *schrunds* half-opening their icicle eyelids to the heavens. Cold curdled névé poured down on all sides between jutting walls of splintered rock. Sometimes we mounted ruins of avalanches, using the frozen balls as helpful steps. Then we came to a hard slope where the whispers of baby breezes were silenced by the crunch of Carrel's axe.

On the farthest southern horizon domed clouds were rising in upward air-currents like great plane trees. At last only one glacier rift, though it was 50 yards (46 metres) wide at least and more like a valley than a shroud, remained to be turned, before easy snow-slopes, interrupted by two insignificant *bergschrunds*, offered kindly access to the col on the arête joining the Aiguille Grise to the Dôme du Goûter's southward ridge. After three hours of ascent up the glacier we halted for breakfast fifteen minutes below this col.

A cold wind caught us on the ridge. At first we hardly noticed it, for we were warm with walking and the view was grand. Divinely blue was our glimpse of Geneva's lake, whilst all the lower hills

This is the graceful Aiguille de Bionnassay seen from the slopes of the Dôme du Goûter on the regular route up Mont Blanc from the Goûter Hut. Conway's party would have passed close by here having reached the ridge at the Col de Bionnassay.

RIGHT: Ian Howell is seen on the South Face of the Barre des Écrins, the highest peak in the Dauphiné and thus the most westerly 4,000-m peak in the Alps. Exactly 99 years after its first ascent we found this classic mixed route – a climb on rock, snow and ice – quite awkward owing to the shrinking glacier and an icefield that had virtually disappeared. I was hit by rockfall and was lucky not have been seriously injured. As it was, we were forced to endure a miserable bivouac on the descent while contemplating global warming.

spread beneath a purple haze. Dauphiné too saluted us, and the country through which we had come – Ruitor and Sassière, Grand Paradis, Levanna, and Grande Casse, Monte Viso, and ranges more remote.

A comfortably broad snow arête led in a few minutes to the point of junction with that from the Aiguille de Bionnassay, whose slender edge trended gracefully away. In three-quarters of an hour we reached the narrow crest, whence, by a sudden breaking storm, Count Villanova and his guides were blown to swift destruction, so that their bodies have since remained undiscovered in the depth of the glacier below. But today, though the wind was cold, it was not too strong for safety. Besides, truth to tell, the arête at its narrowest is not really narrow. Had we not heard of its fame we should have passed it unnoticed.

As the morning advanced the atmosphere grew more dense with vapour and more rich in hue. Flocks of tiny oval clouds grazed the green hills. The Lake of Geneva was lost beneath a purple pall. The snow sometimes gave place to ice, which delayed our advance and made step-cutting laborious, and this was especially the case when we reached the flank of the Dôme. There, too, the wind rose and smote us fiercely, when, in an hour-and-a-quarter from the Col de Bionnassay, we emerged on the broad saddle by the Dôme, twenty minutes below Monsieur Vallot's huts.

Moonrise over the northern slopes of the Dôme du Gôuter, bathed in alpenglow for the few moments before night prevails. The view is from the Grands Mulets Hut to which Conway descended from Mont Blanc summit.

There are two of these, one built for the use of climbers, the other for the owner's accommodation and observatory. Some excellent scientific work has already been accomplished here. It looks a more business-like affair than the hut on the summit of the peak, built in imitation of it by Monsieur Jansen, and which could scarcely have been built at all but for the accommodation provided for the workmen by the Vallot Hut. Monsieur Vallot is therefore evidently within his rights when he claims to be the pioneer in the matter of Mont Blanc observatories.

We sheltered a while behind the *cabane* and quitted our baggage there, when Karbir, Aymonod and I started to cut steps up the exposed ridge of the Bosses, leaving the others to follow at their warmth and leisure. Karbir led to the summit and did all the cutting quickly and well. We had no predecessors' tracks to abbreviate our toil. The area of the view steadily enlarged, but the amount of visible earth diminished under the cloudflocks, which gathered into beautiful lines, long drawn out, one beyond another.

The panorama was complete and included the Pennine and Oberland ranges besides those we had already seen. It was, however, the clouds that fascinated us most, the flocks of little ones on the hills at our feet and the lines of soft white billows as it were breaking far away on a wide and shallow shore, with blue between and beneath them. Far to the south, creamy in sunlight and distance, rose domed cumuli above the Maritimes. Everything looked still, and yet, I suppose, the wind was really hurrying along the air and whatever floated within it. The sky for a quarter of its height had parted with its azure to the valley-deeps and was striped all round with finest lines, incredibly numerous, like the lines in a

The Aiguille du Midi is the highest of the celebrated Chamonix Aiguilles, that cluster of sharp granite peaks rising steeply over the town – the undisputed hub of modern alpinism. Bill O'Connor is seen descending one of the pinnacles that grace the Éperon Cosmiques, a climb deservedly popular thanks to its easy access from the cable car which lifts tourists to the mountain's summit.

wide-stretched solar spectrum, and each edging a new grade of tone.

We ran in half an hour back to the Vallot Hut, picked up our things, and made off for Chamonix by the well-known way. As we dipped to the Grand Plateau, the snow began to be soft, but it never became really bad. We turned the crevasse below the Plateau by its left end, ran easily down the slope called Grandes Montées, and hurried across the Petit Plateau, where men have lost their lives and will again lose them in the ice-avalanches that, from time to time, tumble from the Dôme du Goûter's cliffs and sweep the whole breadth of the traversable way. The steep snow-slope of the Petites Montées was too soft to be glissaded; down it we had to wade and then find our way through the crevassed region that intervenes between it and the Grands Mulets. Here, with no tracks to guide us, we might have lost some time, but our men were skilful and fortunate, so that, in an hour-and-three-quarters from the Vallot hut, we reached the edge of the rocks by the well-known Grands Mulets cabane (10,010 feet/3,051 metres) and were rejoiced to find it occupied.

*Early morning is a magical time in the Alps. This
picture shows the Wetterhorn, the mountain whose
ascent by Sir Alfred Wills in 1854 is held to mark the
opening of the Golden Age of alpine mountaineering.
It rises sheer more than 5,000ft (1,600 m) above the
shadowed saddle of Grosse Scheidegg at the eastern
head of the Lütschental – the Grindelwald valley. My
climbing mate stands on the narrow Mittellegi Hörnli,
the shoulder on the Eiger's North East or Mittellegi
Ridge from where this famous climb is usually started.*

JUNGFRAU

The light from the lowering moon was decorating the view with sharply-edged bars of light and cones of shadow cast by the white hills; but the moon was gone by the time we started and only the lanterns of two parties, an hour-and-a-half ahead, twinkled like orange stars on the vague floor. Silence reigned in the still air. Descending a gully full of loose stones, we entered the ice, and crossed the foot of the Grünhorn Glacier, which we were to mount the next day to the col at its head.

The recently fallen snow upon the ice was not hard enough frozen to bear our weight, but this unpleasantness did not last, and, as we advanced below the foot of the Ewig Schnee Feld's broad icefield and up the Jungfrau Firn's left side, the surface was firm and crisp beneath our feet. What beautiful names the mountains and glaciers have in this region – the Maiden, the Monk, the Ogre, the Dark Eagle Peak, the Bright Eagle, the Peak of Storms, the Peak of Terror, the Field of Everlasting Snow – how much better than Mount Jones or Mount Mackenzie!

The upper part of the Jungfraufirn falls in swelling terraces from its encircling peaks and ridges. At each bend, open or covered crevasses are numerous and have to be carefully negotiated. Shrieks from one of the parties we left behind informed us that a man had fallen into a hole and was in process of being hauled out. There was no reason to shriek, and, indeed, every reason not to do so, for help was not required and we might easily have been betrayed into going back. As it was, we had to halt till we could be sure that they were continuing their way. Excitable novices are a nuisance on a mountain, especially when they are led, as in this case, by bad guides. Good and careful guides seldom fall into crevasses. They discover and avoid them. The process takes a little time, but the discomfort of being hauled out of a crevasse is worth avoiding.

The first grey indication of dawn, rendering our lanterns needless, seemed to come up simultaneously all round the horizon. It was not long before a bed of orange light gave colour to the sky in the south-east. When we reached the highest level of the glacier, some way below the Jungfrau Joch, and were bending round to the west, the Jungfrau suddenly blushed a faint pink over all its rocky face, then grew pale, blushed again, and finally, waxing golden, shone for some minutes in

The beautiful Jungfrau (aptly meaning "maiden") forms part of the Bernese Oberland – the great rampart that fronts the Bernese Alps. The northern flank of the mountain is seen here from the meadows of Kleine Scheidegg.

singular glory before white daylight reigned. Aymonod was unusually happy all the morning. His love of glacier scenery found continual satisfaction. "What beauty! What beauty!" he kept exclaiming; "is it not a pleasure to walk thus? There is indeed no difficulty for a climber here, but difficulty is not everything. Look at the Aiguilles of Chamonix, for example; they are difficult enough, but as points of view they are miserable. Here, look where we may, there is beauty on every side."

Few ascents in the Alps are simpler than that of the Jungfrau from the south for people who understand mountains. There is none better worth making. Immediately south of the peak is a snowy saddle, called the Rottalsattel, and south of that again the Roththalhorn, a rocky hump, which sends a snow-ridge eastwards into the glacier. Between this snow-ridge and the north-east ridge of the Jungfrau there is hidden a deep bay or theatre, with walls and floor of purest snow: a lovely retreat where some glacier fairy dwells, uncumbered by views of the lower world. Ice cliffs impend on either hand and occasionally cast down avalanches. A steep slope at the end leads up to the Rottalsattel, and I should think that sometimes this slope may be in dangerous condition, when the ascent or descent might better be made by the aforesaid white ridge, which can easily be reached both from the Sattel and the névé below. I understand that, in some years, this is the route generally followed by the Eggishorn guides.

ABOVE: Evening light on the Chamonix Aiguilles, from the old moraines below the Nantillons Glacier. On the left rise Charmoz and Grépon; in the centre is Blaitière; while the Aiguille du Plan, Deux Aigles, Pélerins and Peigne stand on the right.

BELOW: The approach to the Rottalsattel, from Concordia, lies up this bay of the Jungfraufirn, from where a steep couloir breaks through the great seracs already bathed in dawn alpenglow. Conway came this way on his Jungfrau ascent.

The Jungfrau summit rises above a swirling cloud-sea. I took this picture from the north-east, on the summit of the Mönch (13,448ft/ 4,099m), before starting a swift descent in the face of the breaking weather.

We pounded our way up the slope, crossed a *bergschrund* at the top of it by a good snow-bridge, and so gained a little snowy plateau, just below the Rottal-sattel and protected from the north-west wind that was blowing on the actual col. We made our first halt at this point, after four hours' easy walking from the hut, and were perfectly happy and comfortable. The whole day was before us; the scenery was superb. Higher up there would be wind. As Aymonod had made the steps so far, I decided that the guides of the other parties should cut them up the arête. We halted for two hours to let them pass, and then made the mistake of following too soon. Our fellow climbers were not experienced, and their guides, doubtless wisely, cut for them a staircase of deep ledges like armchairs.

Two climbers, Tess Burrows and Clive Booth, pause on the upper slopes of the Jungfrau's South Ridge above the Rottalsattel. This section is quite exposed and often sheathed in hard blue ice – as Conway himself discovered. It is late September, the end of the season, and, in the far distance, the Finsteraarhorn rise from a characteristic autumnal cloud-sea.

Such step-cutting, in blue ice, was necessarily slow. We followed impatiently, restrained by Aymonod's good manners from cutting round and snatching the first place again. The method of progress of one of our companions was this. His leading guide, having enlarged to a preposterous size the already large steps made by the first party, sat down and hoisted his employer up to him by the rope. He then went forward five steps, repeated the process, and so on.

At last we reached the crest of broken rocks close to the summit, and in a few moments were on the top, with a cold breeze freezing the marrow of our bones. We only halted long enough to fasten in the memory the small remainder of the view which had not been visible from the arête.

The Jungfrau's panorama is one of the most famous in the Alps, and in some respects its fame is deserved. The distant view is excellently composed, for the

This panorama was shot eastwards from the Obermönchjoch as the alpenglow lingered on the twin peaks of the Schreckhorn and Lauteraarhorn. The moon rose and frost gripped my fingers. The Wetterhorn is seen on the left and the upper basin of the Ewig-schneefeld Glacier below.

great ranges visible are concentrated into groups. Mont Blanc looks surpassingly fine and of more imposing magnitude than from many a nearer summit. A panorama, however, depends much on the nature of the foreground for its effect, for the foreground occupies nine-tenths of the visible area. A glance at the map would suggest that the Jungfrau is singularly favoured in this respect, for it stands at the edge of the region of lakes and wooded hills whereof Interlaken is the centre, whilst on the other side it appears to look down the greatest of Alpine glaciers.

Unfortunately, as a minuter examination of the map reveals, in neither of these respects is it entirely blessed. Its own protruding shoulders, the Silberhorn on the one hand and the Schneehorn on the other, prevent the sight from plunging into the Vale of Lauterbrunnen and cut off a part of the Wengern Alp, whilst southwards the Aletsch Glacier is so placed that its length and splendour are disguised. The position of the peak awakens expectations which it fails to satisfy. The climber hopes to look down a splendid series of precipitous snow- and ice-slopes, into a deep and fertile valley, to behold blue lakes beyond, and then wooded hills rolling away to a remote distance. On the other side he expects to command the finest névé basin in the Alps and to trace a great ice-river pouring from it. Such a view would be of unusual beauty. But the plunge is not there. The lakes are for the most part hidden, whilst the snowy area is indifferently seen, the near mountains are badly grouped and of undignified forms, and the ice-river vanishes round a corner far too soon. Perhaps the view from the Mönch is better, though I suspect that there the Trugberg interrupts the sublime simplicity of the Aletsch Glacier's curve.

Our descent from the col to the hut was a featureless grind. We minimised the toil through the soft snow by going as slowly as we pleased, halting sometimes to drink at pools or runlets of ice-cold water, sometimes to smoke a pipe and give ourselves to the enjoyment of the beautiful scenery, whereof one is apt to become oblivious in the hot hours of afternoon. We reached the hut after two hours and a half of leisurely walking, and found FitzGerald still deep in a refreshing sleep and Larden long ago returned from a successful but cold ascent of the Finsteraarhorn. Our men, returning from the Eggishorn, brought the materials for soup and other creature comforts. We retired early to our bed-shelf and a good night's rest, which was, truth to tell, not unpleasantly disturbed by the rattle of hail on the roof over our heads.

A rope of climbers ascends the easy upper slopes of the Ewigschneefeld Glacier towards the Obermönchjoch – the broad saddle between the Mönch and the sharp-looking Trugberg seen in this picture.

This is a panorama over the Bernese Alps from the
Jungfrau summit. On the left stand the northern faces
of Ebnefluh, Mittaghorn, Grosshorn and the Lauter-
brunnen Breithorn. The sunlit peak in the centre is the
Tschingelhorn. Nearest in the line of peaks on the right
is the Gspaltenhorn. Then, each with an ice-face to the
northwest, are Blümlisalp, Doldenhorn, Balmhorn and
Altels. The horizon shows the Pennines – Matterhorn,
Weisshorn, Dent d'Hérens and Dent Blanche. Grand
Combin and Mont Blanc are in the centre-horizon.

THE WESTERN ALPS – FACTFILE

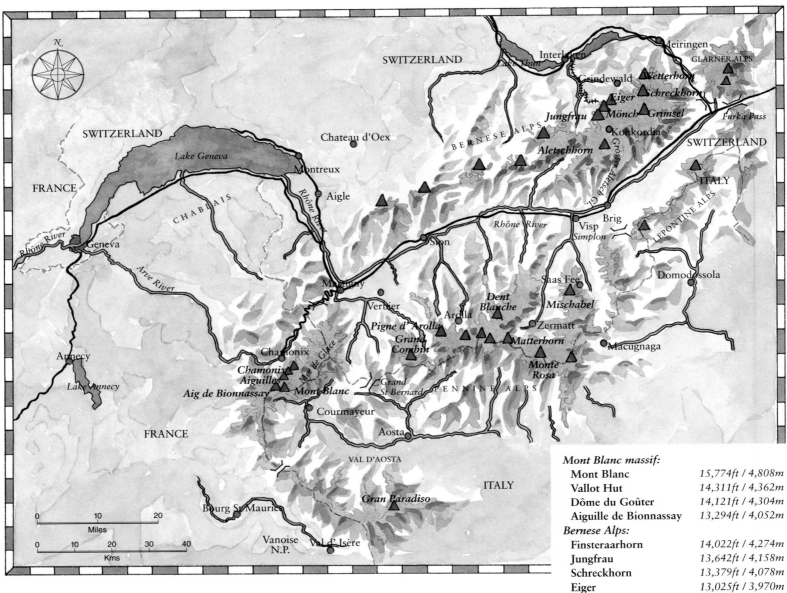

Mont Blanc massif:	
Mont Blanc	*15,774ft / 4,808m*
Vallot Hut	*14,311ft / 4,362m*
Dôme du Goûter	*14,121ft / 4,304m*
Aiguille de Bionnassay	*13,294ft / 4,052m*
Bernese Alps:	
Finsteraarhorn	*14,022ft / 4,274m*
Jungfrau	*13,642ft / 4,158m*
Schreckhorn	*13,379ft / 4,078m*
Eiger	*13,025ft / 3,970m*
Wetterhorn	*12,152ft / 3,704m*
Pennine Alps:	
Matterhorn	*14,690ft / 4,478m*
Dauphiné:	
Barre des Écrins	*13,455ft / 4,101m*
Eastern Graians:	
Gran Paradiso	*13,323ft / 4,061m*
Vanoise:	
Grande Casse	*12,638ft / 3,852m*

BACKGROUND

Comprising dozens of sub-ranges, the many folds of the European Alps spring from the Mediterranean coast behind Monaco, arc around northern Italy and, after some 650 miles (1,000km), fade away into the Balkan highlands. The Western Alps are the mountains of France, Switzerland and Italy, that are west and south of the Simplon and Grimsel passes.

All but one of the 52 alpine summits above 13,123ft (4,000m) rise here – most of them above sizeable glaciers. The largest and most important sub-ranges are the Mont Blanc massif, the Pennine Alps and the Bernese Alps. Mountaineering as a sport was born here between 1854 and 1865 – the so-called Golden Age of Mountaineering, when adventurous Victorian gentlemen (usually English) and their locally recruited guides first reached virtually

In the summer the Alps are new again and the ski-mountaineer embarks on a voyage of rediscovery. After overnight snow skiers ascend towards the Tsena Refien Glacier towards the Col de Serpentine and the Pigne d'Arolla, a stage on the famous Chamonix to Zermatt Haute Route.

all the major summits. Ever since, the Alps have been the crucible of world mountaineering, the home of ski-mountaineering and the mecca of downhill skiers.

ACCESS

Mountain sport, its several manifestations including alpinism, skiing and hiking, is virtually a national pastime in Switzerland, France, Italy, Austria and Germany. In Europe no formalities are required to venture into the mountains – climbers and hikers just turn up and go – although appropriate insurance cover against rescue costs and membership of an alpine club giving preferential use of huts are advised. Access is easy to mountains that elsewhere would be considered quite high, thanks to excellent public transport, fine mountain roads, dozens of friendly resort villages, a proliferation of cable-car systems and a comprehensive chain of strategic and well-equipped mountain huts, often in the most unlikely locations. Tourism is highly developed; indeed the number of people in Switzerland doubles during the ski season.

Each alpine centre – as well as certain non-alpine countries such as Britain – has its own corps of professional and highly qualified mountain guides, a tradition that goes back to pioneering days. Guides will lead climbs of all standards and usually also off-piste or ski touring parties in winter.

While all the mountain activities mentioned – and others such as parapenting and mountain biking – are practised throughout the year, the prime climbing season in the Western Alps runs from late June into September, culminating in August. Ski-mountaineers and ski-tourers favour the spring-snow months of April and May. But notwithstanding their popularity, the Alpine mountains are high, savage and dangerous; the glaciers are crevassed; the rock is not always good; and storms can strike at any time.

HIKING AND CLIMBING

Trekkers will find a network of footpaths below the snowline, many leading from hut to hut and sometimes crossing less hazardous snowfields and glaciers. Frequently waymarked, most will be well described in guidebooks in many languages. Alpinists meanwhile enjoy an incredible choice of climbs from straightforward snow plods on worthy summits to desperate multi-day epics on rock or ice as challenging as any in the world. Guidebooks document virtually every route throughout the Alps. Chamonix and the Mont Blanc Range with its prolific mechanical uplift, its typically excellent granite and high-altitude ice – at a time when glaciers are receding throughout the Alps – is something of a forcing centre for modern high-standard climbing. The atmosphere is at times overtly competitive. Every conceivable item of equipment is obtainable in the town. More traditional values still pertain in the less popular Bernese Alps.

The Undiscovered Country

The Western Highlands and Isles of Scotland

W. H. MURRAY

"*I have been a hundred times to the top of Buchaille Etive Mor in Glencoe. In unwise and sentimental moments I am inclined to think of it as an old friend. But I know full well that the next time I go there the Buachaille will surprise me for the hundred and first time – my climb will be unlike any that I have had before.*"

MOUNTAINEERING IN SCOTLAND

The exploratory urge moves every man who loves hills. The quest of the mountaineer is knowledge. He is drawing close to one truth about mountains when at last he becomes aware that he *will* never know them fully – not in all their aspects – nor ever fully know his craft. Like the true philosopher, the true mountaineer can look forward with rejoicing to an eternity of endeavour: to real-isation without end. I have climbed for fifteen years and have hopes of another forty, but I know that my position at the close of my span will be the same as it is now, and the same as it was on that happy day when I first set foot on a hill – the Scottish Highlands will spread out before me, an unknown land.

The yearning to explore hills was born in myself in 1934, when I, a confirmed pavement-dweller, overheard a mountaineer describe a weekend visit to An Teallach in Ross-shire. He spoke of a long thin ridge, 3,000 feet (900 metres) up, with towers and pinnacles and tall cliffs on either flank, which fell to deep corries. And from these corries clouds would boil up like steam from a cauldron, and from time to time shafts would open through them to reveal vistas of low valleys and seas and distant islands. That was all he said, but the effect on myself was profound, because for the first time in my life my exploratory instincts began to stir. Here was a strange new world of which I had never even dreamed, waiting for exploration. And unlike so many other dreams, this was one that could be

This is An Teallach on a sullen winter day seen westwards from the Dirrie More – the main watershed of Scotland – some 15 miles (24km) distant. The name, which translates from the Gaelic as "The Forge", is possibly due to the cloud that characteristically boils in its three great corries, or the dawn alpenglow on the great cliffs of Torridonian Red Sandstone.

realised in action. At the first opportunity, then, I went to one of the few mountains I knew by name – the Cobbler at Arrochar. It was a fine April day, with
plenty of snow on the tops. When I stood by the road at Arrochar and looked
up at my first mountain, the summit seemed alarmingly craggy and blinding
white against blue sky. How I should ever get up I could not imagine. I
picked out a route by the line of a burn, which vanished towards a
huge corrie under the summit rocks. And what then? I felt a nervous hesitation about my fate in these upper regions. Had I been
entering the sanctuary of Nanda Devi I could have felt no more of
the sheer thrill of adventure than I did when I stepped off the road on
to the bare hillside.

*Glencoe: on the North East
Ridge of Stob Coire nan
Lochan (the "Peak of the
Corrie of the Lochans",
3,657ft/1,115m), an outlier
of Bidean nam Bian on the
south side of the glen.*

ABOVE: *Ben Lomond, at 3,192ft (974m), is the most southerly of the Munros, the currently 284 separate Scottish mountains topping 3,000ft (900m). The mountain offers a popular and straightforward ascent with fine views, and it rises over the banks of Loch Lomond, within easy reach of the Glasgow conurbation. This is the final section of the South East Ridge with the summit rising ahead.*

FAR RIGHT: *Approaching the summit of the Cobbler or Ben Arthur from the South Peak: Loch Long – an arm of the sea – lies far below. Although it is only 2,900ft (884m) in height, this is the most popular peak of the Arrochar Alps, thanks to its bizarre craggy form.*

Later in the day, when I entered the Cobbler corrie, I recognised that I *had* entered what was, for me, true sanctuary – a world of rock and snow and glossy ice, shining in the spring sun, and for a moment at least, laughing in the glint and gleam of the world's joy. I too laughed in my sudden awareness of freedom. Had I thought at all I should have said: "Here is a field of free action in which nothing is organised, or made safe or easy by uniform regulation; a kingdom where no laws run and no useful ends fetter the heart." I did not have to think that out in full. I knew it instantaneously, in one all-comprehending glance.

And, of course, this intoxicated me. For it was a great day in my life. And at once I proceeded to do all those wicked things so rightly denounced by grey-bearded gentlemen sitting at office desks in remote cities. I climbed steep snow-slopes by myself. Without an ice-axe or nailed boots, without map, compass, or warm and windproof clothing, and, what is worse, without a companion, I kicked steps up hard snow, going quite fast and gaily, until near the top I stopped and looked down. The corrie floor was now far below me, and black boulders projected out of the snow. If I slid off nothing would stop me until I hit something. I went on with exaggerated caution until I breasted the ridge between the centre and south peaks.

At that first success a wave of elation carried me up high walls of sun-washed rock to the south peak. That rock had beauty in it. Always before I had thought of rock as a dull mass. But this rock was living rock, pale grey and clean as the air itself, with streaks of shiny mica and white crystals of quartzite. It was joy to handle such rock and to feel the coarse grain under the fingers.

Near the top the strangeness of the new environment overawed me a little – nothing but bare rock and boundless space and a bright cloud sailing. Nothing here but myself and the elements – and a knowledge of my utter surrender to and trust in God's providence, and a gladness in that knowledge. On the flat rocks on top I sat down, and for an hour digested all that had happened to me. In being there at all I had, of course, sinned greatly against all the canons of mountaineering. But I did not know that. This was my Garden of Eden stage of purest innocence. It was not till later, when I plucked my apple in search of knowledge, that I read in text-books, "Man must not go alone on mountains" – not when he is a bootless novice. Meantime I looked out upon the mountains circling me in a white-topped throng, and receding to horizons that rippled against the sky like a wash of foam. Not one of these hills did I know by name, and every one was probably as worth exploring as the Cobbler. The shortness of life was brought home to me with a sudden pang. However, what I lacked in time might in part be offset by unflagging activity. From that day I became a mountaineer.

Upon returning home and consulting books I learned that there are 543 mountain-tops in Scotland above 3,000 feet (900 metres). They cannot all be climbed in one's first year. This thought made me feel frustrated. I once received a book after waiting long and eagerly for its publication. Like a wolf coming

ABOVE: Sgurr a'
Chaorachain (2,598ft/
792m) displaying its great
pinnacled Cioch Buttress –
a fine climb – as seen
southwards from
neighbouring Beinn Bhan.
The Cuillin mountains of
Skye and Rhum lie on the
horizon behind the figure.

RIGHT: Cairntoul (4,241ft/
1,293m) rises beyond the
Garbh Choire – the highest
corrie in Britain – from
Braeriach. There is said to
have been a relict glacier
here as late as the early
eighteenth century.

down starving from the mountains, I gulped the courses in any order, reading the end first, snatching bits in the middle running here and there through the pages in uncontrolled excitement. I wanted to know it all immediately. In the end I was sufficiently exhausted to read whole chapters at a time. That was exactly how I felt about mountains. In my first year I sped all over Scotland – going alone because I knew no one else who climbed – snatching mountains here, there and everywhere. As it happened I could not have made a better approach. The best and natural way of dealing with mountains is the way I luckily followed: before starting any rock-climbing I spent a summer and winter on hill-walking only. Rockclimbing, as a means of penetrating the inmost recesses and as sport, should not come until later. Thus I made a wide reconnaissance by climbing several peaks in each of the main mountain districts. This preliminary survey gave me a good idea of their differences in character, which are surprisingly wide, and showed what each had to offer.

When I went from the rolling plateaux and snow-domes of the Cairngorms, mounted among broad forests and straths, to the sharp spiky ridges of Wester Ross, set between winding sea-lochs, I had the sensation peculiar to entering a foreign country; a sense not to be accounted for by any material changes in scenery, but one that is nonetheless shared by all men. I can travel from Inverness to Sussex and feel only that I have moved from one part of Britain to another. But Wester Ross is another (and better) land. Again, when I came from the Cuillin pinnacles and the stark isles of the west to the heathery swell of the southern highlands I returned from vertical desert to grassland, although still hungering like a camel after its dear desert. Between such different areas Glencoe and Lochaber held a fair balance. They had everything: peak, plateau, precipice, the thinnest of ridges, and green valley, all set between the wildest of wild moors and a narrow sea loch – they were Baghdad and Samarkand, at once home and the goal of the pilgrim.

Then I joined a mountaineering club. For the course of that first year's wanderings showed plainly that no man can have the freedom of mountains unless he can climb on rock and snow. The mountains are under snow for several months of the year. Indeed, they excel in winter, offering a sport and beauty quite different from those of summer, a sport harder and tougher, and a more simple and pure beauty. The plateaux and the summit ridges, the great cliffs and the snow-slopes, these are four facets of the Scottish mountains, none of which can be avoided, except the cliffs and these only if a man is content to walk on mainland tops. In the Cuillin of Skye the rocks are not a facet, they *are* the mountains. Cliffs must not be thought of as blank cliffs. They are cathedral cities with many a spire, tower, turret, pinnacle and bastion, amongst which a man may wander at will, and explore and adventure, upon which he may test qualities of character and skill, and by aid of which conquer nothing except himself.

In succeeding years the wider my experience grew the more clearly did I see that however much I might explore this unknown country called the Scottish Highlands, I should never plumb the Unknown. To know mountains we must know them at the four seasons, on the four facets, at the four quarters of the day. The permutations are infinite. For the variations in snow and ice and weather conditions are inexhaustible. No winter climb, say, on the north face of Nevis, is ever the same twice running. If we go to the Comb of Arran in autumn frost, on a day of still, crisp air when distant moors flame red through a sparkle of hoar, we shall not recognise it as the mountain we knew when clouds were scudding

An autumn view down the Nevis Gorge that links upper and lower Glen Nevis. The peak rising in the distance is Carn Dearg – South West to distinguish it from no less than five other Carn Deargs (Red Cairns) in the Nevis massif – a mere excrescence on the huge southern flank of Ben Nevis, the tallest hillside in the country.

along the crags and the hail drove level. I have been a hundred times to the top of Buachaille Etive Mor in Glencoe. In unwise and sentimental moments I am inclined to think of it as an old friend. But I know full well that the next time I go there the Buachaille will surprise me for the hundred and first time – my climb will be unlike any that I've had before.

Treasures of reality yet unknown await discovery among inaccessible peaks at the ends of the earth, still more on the old and familiar peaks at our very doorstep, most of all within each mountaineer. The truth is that in getting to know mountains he gets to know himself. That is why men truly live when they climb.

TWENTY-FOUR HOURS ON THE CUILLIN

It was ten o'clock at night, in Glen Brittle. The June sun had left our little cluster of tents, which nestled behind a screen of golden broom between the Atlantic and the Cuillin. Eastward, the peaks were written along the sky in a high, stiff hand. High above us, the brown precipice of Sron na Ciche, which reacts, chameleon-like, to every subtle change of atmosphere, was dyed a bright blood-red in the setting sun.

I watched the lights fade from the rocks and white evening mist begin to creep round the hills, then I thought of having supper and retiring with a pipe to my sleeping-bag. But in this hope I had reckoned without my friend, B.H. Humble; his head, adorned by a dilapidated panama, emerged of a sudden from the door

It is midsummer and snow patches still linger as two hill-walkers approach the Carn Mor Dearg summit (the "Big Red Cairn", 4,012ft/1,223m) on the celebrated ridge traverse via the Carn Mor Dearg Arête round to Ben Nevis, whose summit and 1,800-ft (550-m) North East Buttress are seen to the right.

Britain's highest mountain, Ben Nevis (4,406ft/1,343m) – the "Vicious" or "Malicious Ben" – dominates the northern horizon in this winter view from Creise in the Blackmount massif. On the left is the East Face of Buachaille Etive Mor (the "Great Shepherd of Etive"), guarding the portal of Glencoe.

of a nearby tent. The lighted eye, the mouth upturned at the corners, the warm colour – they all bore witness to a recent brainstorm. Humble had given birth to an idea. I regarded him with profound suspicion.

"It would be a fine night for a climb," said Humble tentatively. "Well," I hastily replied, "there's going to be no moon, no stars – it will be dark, cold, cloudy, and every cliff in mist. Granted that, it's heresy to deny that all weather's climbing weather."

But Humble was paying no attention to me. "We'd start right now," said he; "go up to Coire Banachdich, rest on the main ridge, then north along the tops."

"And what then?"

"Leave it to me ..." And he looked away very mysteriously.

"On this very spot," I protested, "is to be had a hot meal, a quiet pipe and an eiderdown sleeping-bag." But I was merely according the flesh its privilege of free speech. The spirit was already aloft, I was pulling on my boots ...

I had faith in Humble. He is one of those men who brim with an incalculable alliance of ingenuity and energy. A rock-climb in his company has all the fascination of a mystery tour; one is likely to end, not on some nearby peak, but miles from anywhere in a rarely visited mountain stronghold. And if port be not made until all hours of the day and night, at least one returns buoyed by novelties and ballasted by exhaustion. Of one thing I felt certain: there was more to his taciturnity than met the eye. I knew him. What that "more" might be I should have to wait for time to disclose. I packed a rucksack, picked up a rope, and we bade farewell to Maitland and Higgin, the two remaining members in our party.

A June gloaming in Skye is so drawn-out that one may usually climb on moderate rocks until eleven o'clock. But the mist had been brewing for an hour in the corries and now overflowed round every peak, complicating the problem of route-selection through the wilderness of screes and boulders that carpet Coire Banachdich. Up the wall that backs the corrie a winding route gives easy access to the main ridge. To find that route in mist at late twilight was another matter. Indeed it proved to be impossible.

We climbed the face by guess and by God a considerable height towards the crest, until an unavoidable traverse brought us to a square rock platform, like a balcony. The situation had a dramatic aspect that appealed to us. Below, the rocks plunged into blackness; above, they rose sheer into the mysteries of the mist. We resolved to bivouac until there was sufficient light for safe climbing. There was just enough room on the ledge to accommodate us in comfort. Like difficulty, comfort on mountains is a term relative to the individual climber. We could stretch out at full length, heads pillowed on a rope or rucksack. The rock made an indifferent mattress and night cloud a chill blanket, but luckily I have the capacity to sleep at will, any time and anywhere, and

This is the classic view of the Black Cuillin mountains of Skye as seen from Elgol over the waters of (sea) Loch Scavaig. The saw-tooth ridge, which runs unbroken for nearly 8 miles (13km) from the peak on the left, Gars-Bheinn ("Echoing Mountain"; 2,935ft/895m), is silhouetted against the luminous midsummer dusk.

> *Weariness*
> *Can snore upon the flint, when resty sloth*
> *Finds the down pillow hard.*

Humble wakened me at two AM. The darkness was appreciably less but mist still enveloped us. We could now see to move, and in ten minutes arrived on the rim of the main ridge at about 3,000 feet (900 metres). We turned northward and scrambled over the three tops of Sgurr na Banachdich. Immediately beyond Banachdich the ridge takes a big swing north-east, the first curve of the horseshoe that encloses Coruisk. The route at this juncture was by no means easy to find; four ridges branch downward-bound, and it is only too easy to follow the wrong line. The compass, moreover, is untrustworthy, for magnetic rocks on Banachdich attract the needle.

After reconnaissance we saw close by the pike of Sgurr Thormaid, projecting like a dragon's fang through streamers of twisting cloud. We swarmed up one side and down the other, secure in the knowledge that our route was now correct. A traverse of the Cuillin ridge in mist is a stirring experience. The jagged edge, picturesque enough when clear, then astounds the eye with a succession of distorted towers. They impend suddenly through the clouds, grim, as wild in outline as any creation of nightmare.

At three AM, we reached Sgurr a' Greadaidh. The dawn was well under way and sunrise might shortly be expected. Nothing was visible save mist, so we halted to cheer ourselves with a bite of food. I confess that I again fell asleep, curled up on a slab that gently tilted me over the southern cliff. In a short while Humble roused me. He was justifiably in a state of high excitement. On every hand the mist was sinking, and slowly, one by one, each peak of the Cuillin reared a black tip through snow-white vapour.

Never again in summer have I seen a sight so magnificent. The clouds had now fallen to a uniform level at 2,500 feet (750 metres); just sufficient to hide the linking ridges and to isolate each pinnacle of the 6-mile (9.5-kilometre) horseshoe. From the mainland to far beyond the Outer Hebrides this cloud-mass formed an unbroken sea. Immediately between our feet the surface surged and spun as though impelled by inner vortices, rising and falling like the rollers of a mid-Atlantic swell. Over the submerged cols between each mountain the ocean poured and seethed in a never-ending flow.

The grey sky was steadily changing to cornflower blue and black rock to ashen. To obtain a still finer vantage point we moved east to Sgurr a' Mhadaidh. No sooner did we reach the top than the sun rose. Down in the basin of Coruisk, the cloud-surface at once flashed into flame, as though a stupendous crucible were filled with burning silver. The twenty turrets of the Cuillin, like islands lapped by fire-foam, flushed faintly pink. The shade crimsoned. Within a space of minutes, the rocks had run the gamut of autumn leafage, "yellow, and black, and pale, and hectic red".

Beyond such bare words one may say little. The mind fails one miserably and painfully before beauty. It cannot understand. Yet it would contain more. Mercifully, it is by this very process of not understanding that one is allowed to understand much; for each one had within him "the divine reason that sits at the helm of the soul", of which the head knows nothing. However, I must be content to observe that here for the first time, broke upon me the unmistakable intimation of a last reality underlying mountain beauty; and here, for the

Doing the Dubhs (see caption, p.52) is the most classic of Skye scrambles. The crux is the descent from Sgurr Dubh Beag (the "Little Black Peak"), usually achieved by abseil. Alternatively, my friend, the guide Rusty Baillie, descends hand over hand down the rope – a technique not really to be recommended!

first time, it awakened within me a faculty of comprehension that had never before been exercised.

Humble indeed had not failed me. He had hoped for a noble panorama. But in the bleak hours around midnight not even he had dreamed that we should be led by cloud and fire to the land of promise. Since then I have always believed and repeatedly proved that the mountains reserve their fairest prize for the man who turns aside from common-sense routine. One might say that hills repay trust with generosity. In Glen Brittle, our companions when they awoke saw nothing but a steelgrey layer of low clouds, and not imagining that the peaks were in sunlight, commiserated us on such an unprofitable end to our waywardness.

Several of the best hours of our otherwise misspent lives were passed away on Sgurr a' Mhadaidh. Towards nine o'clock the cloud-bank broke up and gradually dissolved. We scrambled down to the high col under Bidein Druim nan Ramh, and thence turned downward towards Coruisk by the Corrie of Solitude. Overhead, hardly a wisp of cloud remained; below, Loch Coruisk was a royal blue rippled with silver.

After winning clear of the screes in the corrie we walked the best part of two miles south, to the junction in the main burn and the loch. And here I add my voice to Humble's in exploding the myth of the "gloomy Coruisk". The face of Scotland has so often been falsified by writers in search of melodrama that there is now difficulty in convincing people of the evidence of their own eyes. Far from being shadowed and overhung by beetling crags, Loch Coruisk has a fairly open situation, inasmuch as the Cuillin main ridge lies a couple of miles back. In spring and summer it is flooded by sunlight for the best part of the day. I have heard it further alleged that here grows no tuft of vegetation; yet when I stood beside the loch with Humble the very banks were alive with wild flowers, their hues offset by cool green shrubs and long grasses. We might have imagined ourselves transported to the land of Xanadu, where

... Twice five miles of fertile ground
With walls and towers were girdled round,
And there were gardens, bright with sinuous rills.

A few of these flowers were rare, and Humble, who is an accomplished botanist, was highly gratified by some carnivorous specimens.

As I am ill content to rejoice in mountains yet not climb them, so I am compelled not only to admire lochs and rivers but to plunge in and swim. In either act knowledge of their charm is extended. Every condition for the ideal swim had here been satisfied, for the sun had more than warmed us on the 4-mile

RIGHT: "Doing the Dubhs" is the traverse of the long, East Ridge of Sgurr Dubh na da Bheinn (the "Black Peak of the Two Tops", 3,078ft/ 938m), a superb expedition that starts from sea level on the shore of Loch Coruisk, ascends almost 1 mile (1.6km) of slabs and glacis to Sgurr Dubh Beag, and then crosses sharp Sgurr Dubh Mor (the "Big Black Peak"; 3,097ft/944m) to finally reach the main Cuillin Ridge at the summit of Dubh na da Bheinn. In this picture Rusty Baillie looks out over Loch Coruisk from the shoulder of Dubh Beag. On the right is Loch Scavaig, while the fine peak of Bla Bheinn (the "Hill of Bloom", 3,044ft/928m) stands on the left side of the horizon.

(6-kilometre) tramp. There was no need to propose a bathe – of one accord we stripped and plunged. The swim was unique in my own experience because all five senses were feasted to the full.

The sharp sting of that first dive cleared at one stroke the fogs of lethargy from the mind – at one stroke the world stood vivid. The corrie was full of sun and the song of the burn, gay with the flash of many colours and the dance of light on the loch, fresh with the scents of the blossom and an aromatic tang of plants in morning air. I drank from the burn and the taste was sweet and lively to the palate. And these good reports, being gathered together in the mind, suddenly fused in image of the beauty we had seen during the supreme hour on Sgurr a' Mhadaidh: so that I knew, what until then I had not known, that the one Beauty pervades all things according to their nature, they having beauty by virtue of participation in it; and that in the degree of realising its presence within us, so is life lived in fullness. The ecstasy of that morning is bright after eight years.

THE WESTERN HIGHLANDS AND ISLES OF SCOTLAND – FACTFILE

BACKGROUND

The Scottish Highlands are western Europe's largest wilderness, a great plateau of largely Pre-Cambrian rocks eroded by ice-sheet and valley glacier into a rich diversity of mountain form. While lacking in stature, these small craggy mountains are unique in beauty and atmosphere, particularly in the west and on the islands, where they often stand above land or sea-lochs and are always close to the ocean.

At current reckoning, Scotland has 284 Munros (separate mountains) and a further 287 tops all above 3,000ft (915 metres). Mountaineering dates back to the 1870s, when Alpine Club members discovered virgin peaks on Skye. The subsequent ascents of the august Scottish Mountaineering Club, founded in 1889, on the cliffs of Ben Nevis and Glencoe marked the birth of climbing per se.

ACCESS

The road network follows the main glens running typically east-west so there are few places more than 10 rugged miles (16km) from a road of sorts. In three places the railway reaches the coast, while ferries ply to every inhabited island. A road bridge has recently been built to Skye. Remote inns and many villages offer plenty of accommodation, and camping is popular. There are no access problems with land belonging to the National or John Muir Trusts (including the areas described in the article). On privately owned mountains, while de facto access rights are traditional, walkers and climbers are unwelcome when deer stalking takes place in early autumn and permission should be obtained locally. The best weather usually occurs in the spring and early summer, and in the autumn.

HILL-WALKING AND CLIMBING

Hill-walking can be enjoyed on almost any mountain, and the long ridges linking many summits, such as the Five Sisters of Kintail or the Mamores, provide superb expeditions. Munro Bagging is popular, although there are

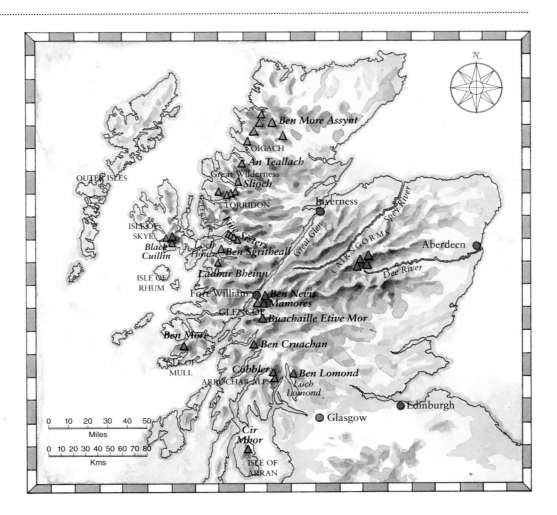

many fine mountains of lesser height. Only An Teallach and the Skye Cuillin demand rock-climbing skills in summer. Snow and ice cloak the mountains in winter, when the weather can be arctic-alpine and real mountaineering skills – at the least, the proficient use of an ice-axe and crampons – are essential. These conditions and the characteristic winter cycle of frost and thaw can provide exceptional ice and mixed climbing of world renown on the abundant cliffs and ridges between the months of December and March.

Although Scottish tradition is more one of mountaineering than technical gymnastics, rockclimbing is well developed, although frequently entails long approach marches to remote cliffs of great character.

Ben Nevis	4,406ft / 1,344m
Ben Macdui	4,296ft / 1,309m
An Teallach	3,484ft / 1,062m
Buachaille Etive Mor	3,345ft / 1,022m
The Cobbler	2,900ft / 884m
Cuillin of Skye:	
Sgurr a' Greadaidh	3,192ft / 973m
Sgurr na Banachdich	3,166ft / 965m
Sgurr Thormaid	3,040ft / 927m
Sgurr a' Mhadaidh	3,012ft / 918m
Druim nan Ramh	2,850ft / 869m
Sron na Ciche	c.2,500ft / 760m

LEFT: *Loch Coruisk, in the heart of the Skye Cuillin. It is surrounded by some 50 sharp rock peaks, many of them rising more than 3,000ft (900m). It is a superb showcase of post-glacial scenery.*

The Light of Other Days

The Canadian Rockies

DAVID HARRIS

*"Above us the ice steepened to vertical, hanging free of the rock, a true
waterfall, frozen in ... time. Last year's precipitation waiting for next
year's heat to continue its course toward the river in the canyon below
us, as if time itself had frozen and stopped. Perhaps that is part of the
attraction: cruising upward over that frozen time I felt exempt from ...
the joys and sorrows that mark and measure human existence,
full to overflowing with the intensity of the moment."*

*This is Mount Robson,
Monarch of the Canadian
Rockies. The Berg Glacier
pours down from the North
Face into remote Berg
Lake. We bivouacked here
by the shore when we came
down from the Kain Face.*

*Oft, in the still of night,
'ere slumber's chains have bound me,
fond memory brings the light
of other days around me.*

It was way past midnight and Fred was sick. He needed sleep. He'd spent the last sixteen hours coughing his ribs loose – ten on the drive from Vancouver with me, and the six before that on a flight from Dallas – but he couldn't force himself to go to bed. He just kept walking around the caboose, touching things – the Victorian wallpaper, the comfortable furniture, the thousands of hardbound books on the built-in bookshelves, the old globe, the antique lamp on the desk.

"A *caboose*! I don't believe this. Where in God's name did they get a caboose?"

For him it must have seemed like we'd timewarped back to the age of steam. For me it was like coming home.

Home Sweet Caboose.

Back in the Canadian Rockies. What more could anyone ask?

*   *   *

How often have I come to these mountains? Twenty times? Thirty? I've lost count. My parents brought me to them for the first time when I was six. Three-and-a-half decades later I brought my own six-year-old son on his first Rockies holiday. And now, another decade down the line, I'm still coming back – albeit in somewhat more luxury since Bruce and Stephanie found this caboose. It has never been clear to me how they managed to get it set up, on a length of track beside their house here in Golden, but set it up they did, and now, renovated, plumbed, wired, decorated, and with a bedroom added, it has become my favorite place. Thank God they tolerate my occasional sojourns here.

*   *   *

We slept in the next morning, and when we finally did get up Fred spent the better part of an hour expectorating things you really don't want to read about. We sat around till noon debating whether it would be safe for him to do anything physical, eventually deciding that, since he'd more or less stopped coughing, we'd drive to one of the nearby roadside ice drools where he could belay while I got a bit of exercise.

It was his first day on ice. He's a gifted rockclimber, but there's not a lot of ice in Texas. He had obviously been nervous as we approached the base of the climb, torn between the desire to try this bizarrely addictive game and the fear of disemboweling himself with the unfamiliar and wickedly sharp crampons and ice tools. Or of falling to his death as the whole

Mount Athabasca rears over the Athabasca tongue of the famous Columbia Icefield – a rare trioceanic watershed, for the Sunwapta River seen here flows to the Arctic Ocean while other tongues drain to the Pacific and to Hudson Bay. There is a glimpse of the Icefields Parkway, the scenic highway linking Banff to Jasper, near the bottom of the picture.

fragile structure we were going to climb gave way underneath us. Or of doing everything right and still paying the ultimate price when some unseen slope above us avalanched.

Two pitches later, hanging from ice screws 100 meters (328 feet) off the deck, he was coughing again, but grinning like he'd found something better than sex. The third pitch looked glorious. A free-hanging curtain of translucent turquoise; seductive, and harder than anything I'd climbed before. Fred was not a well man though, so we rappelled, planning to return the next day.

The next day, however, we took a rain check – literally as well as figuratively. Fred's health had deteriorated and so had the weather. Light snowfall turned to rain as the temperature rose, then the clouds burned off and I began worrying that the sun that was warming Fred back to health was also eating the ice he had

Mount Robson: Bill March crampons his way up the final pitch of the Roof, the steep 300-m (1,000-foot) ice slope at the head of the South East Ridge – itself gained by the famous Kain Face. Above lies only a short section of grotesquely corniced ridge and then the tiny summit – the highest point in the Rockies. This was the route of the first ascent of the mountain in 1913 when the redoubtable Conrad Kain cut more than 600 steps to complete the climb, still considered a North American classic.

come so far to climb. It had been an unusually mild winter, and any ice that faced south was already lean enough without this sudden mad rush into spring.

* * *

Most of my winter trips to the Rockies have truly been excursions into the deep freeze. The first was an eight-day ski traverse along a section of the Continental Divide above the Icefields Parkway. No big deal for an experienced ski mountaineer, but my winter mountaineering experience was limited to a few day trips and I'd never been on skis, so for me it was an all-out adventure. I sympathized with Fred's mixture of fear and anticipation.

Maybe that mixture of emotions is what has kept me coming back for so many years. The Canadian Rockies offer endless scope for the realization of both. It is a mountain range of jaw-dropping contrasts. Roughly the size of the Alps, with about one-thousandth the population, it offers both civilization and remoteness: if the mountains and valleys beside the main roads are not quite as crowded as their European counterparts, neither do they offer any solitude, and Banff, the main outpost of civilization, is a bizarre cross between an alpine village and a suburb of Tokyo. If you want to punctuate your climbing adventures with an evening of chamber music or theater, or if you have a perverse need to be reminded how much less wealthy you are than others, Banff will give you your fix.

But much of the range is empty. Empty of roads, empty of towns, empty of people. About 77,000 square miles (200,000 square kilometers) of peaks and valleys, elk and bears, rock and ice.

* * *

The warmth of Fred's recuperation day had taken a heavy toll on the waterfall. The ice was noticeably thinner now and covered in a 5-centimeter (2-inch) layer of mush that made getting secure crampon placements difficult. He had wanted to try leading, but 5 meters (16 feet) of insecurity changed his mind, and he cleared some of the mush, placed a screw, and lowered down. Taking his place I discovered that good placements were mainly a matter of patience, so I ran the rope out and brought him up. More comfortable on the soft ice after following the first pitch, he led through and we were soon together at our previous day's highpoint.

Fred's diseased lungs were making their condition obvious again, and over the last two hours the weather had disintegrated. Rain fell, mixed with wet snow, turning the ground on the belay ledge into a dirty porridge, soaking our ropes, misting our vision. I thought that given the conditions – his own and the climatic ones – he would want to bail out for the warmth and security of the caboose, but the grin was back and, sick or not, there was no way he would turn back now. I think he'd have gone on even if he was dying. Your first lead on ice has that effect – climbing at its most real.

Above us the ice steepened to vertical, hanging free of the rock, a true

Here we look along the south-west ridge of Pigeon Spire, one of the higher Bugaboos, towards the foreshortened, but still quite steep, headwall below the summit. It's a fairly straightforward climb amid fabulous rock architecture.

waterfall, frozen in place. Frozen in time. Last year's precipitation waiting for next year's heat to continue its course toward the river in the canyon below us, as if time itself had frozen and stopped. Perhaps that is part of the attraction: cruising upward over that frozen time I felt exempt from the rules that regulate and govern the universe, exempt from the joys and sorrows that mark and measure human existence, full to overflowing with the intensity of the moment.

At the top, time began once more to flow around me and I gradually reestablished myself as a participant in the real world. Wet snow was still falling, the valley below me was still full of mist, the muffled sound of the occasional car or truck on the road below reminding me that we were not alone. Still, considering that the road was in fact the Trans Canada Highway, the main artery for commerce and travel in this huge country, I didn't feel particularly impinged upon by civilization.

*   *   *

A wilderness ambience directly above a highway? I couldn't help but contrast that to a late-summer trip of a few years ago. En route to the Rockies, Robb McLaren and I had stopped at the Bugaboos for some climbing on the huge granite peaks that give the area its name. It's a gorgeous place, and its renown as an international mecca of alpine rockclimbing is well deserved. The granite is superb, the peaks – Bugaboo Spire, Snowpatch Spire, Pigeon Spire, the Howser Towers – are spectacular, the approaches are relatively benign, there are routes at all grades, and it's considerably further off the beaten path than the roadside ice climbs near Golden.

An hour off the Trans Canada Highway had taken us to the tiny town of Spillimacheen. Another hour up a steep and twisty gravel road took us as far as we could go on wheels, and a final three hours up a trail brought us to the Kain Hut – and more people, by far, than we'd seen in some of the towns we had passed through. The hut was full to capacity, the surrounding area was an overcrowded tent slum, and, as we discovered the next morning, every route within our ability was swarming with climbers.

We ran for the Rockies, camping the next night at a small lake only a few minutes off the highway. We had the place to ourselves on one of the most beautiful summer evenings I've ever enjoyed. A campsite on a soft carpet of pine needles near the lakeshore, water lapping on a beach of tiny smooth stones, and eventually the dark pines on the far shore silhouetted against the dying purple light … quite a contrast to the "wilderness" of the Bugaboos and a wonderful prelude to several days of sun-blessed climbing on the peaks above the Columbia Icefield.

*   *   *

Getting down off the waterfall was a weather-handicapped race with fading daylight, three rappels on ropes so wet and dirty that mud literally poured out of

them as they passed through my descender. But through it all I was buoyant, ecstatic almost, my spirit soaring as my body sank earthward. Hadn't I just done the most difficult ice lead of my life? And in horrible conditions just like they do in books? And didn't it feel *so* fine to have the needle back in the vein? Okay, okay, given the standards of the day, my lead wasn't exactly newsworthy, but it had been hard for me, and by God it *did* feel good to have the needle back in.

Fred's coughing brought me back to here-and-now. Time to get him home to the caboose where he could put on dry clothes, warm up, rehydrate and dose himself with whatever tablets, capsules, and bottled cough syrups he could lay his hands on – drugs *du jour*. He must have been miserable belaying me on that last pitch. Cold. Wet. Wracked by painful coughing spasms. He was silent for most of the drive back and I felt guilty about feeling good when he must feel like warmed-over death, but the words that came out when he finally spoke were, "I got to that place again."

Seen here from the South Ridge of Bugaboo Spire, the West Face of Snowpatch Spire rises sheer above the Bugaboo Saddle. The base of Pigeon Spire is seen on the right.

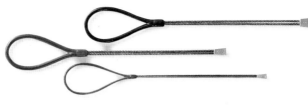

"Huh?"

"The special place at the center where everything goes quiet."

He looked at me and I could tell he was free-floating just as I was. "I haven't been there for a long, long time."

Amazing.

*   *   *

Enthusiastic as he was about the ice, Fred clearly needed time off, so we left our climbing equipment in the caboose the next morning and hit the road with nothing more on our minds than to enjoy as much scenery as we could before the sun set.

The town of Golden is on the extreme western edge of the Rockies, and as we drove east the mountains towering over us gradually changed character. Snow-draped and pyramidal at first, indistinguishable to my non-geologist eyes from the Columbia Mountains to the west, then becoming steeper and more angular, their classic horizontal bedding obvious even under the snow, and finally, as we approached their eastern limit, becoming so vertiginous that snow could no longer cling. No question about how Castle Mountain got its name – with walls and ramparts and turrets like that, what else could it have been called?

We stopped for lunch in Canmore near the eastern side of the range. Which way now? South would take us up and over the pass between Mount Rundle and Chinaman's Peak, then past Spray Lake and into Kananaskis Country with views of Mount Assiniboine (the so-called "Matterhorn of the Rockies") to the west and the golden limestone of the Kananaskis peaks to the east. That would leave us driving back to Golden in the dark (no big deal) and late for the supper that Stephanie had promised to have waiting (a very big deal). Or we could turn back toward Golden now, with a sidetrip up the Icefields Parkway and a chance to see some of the peaks that have put the Canadian Rockies on the climber's map of the world?

Hunger won out, and we headed back west to Lake Louise, then north along the Parkway where, one after another, the great peaks and glaciers floated past, the sight of them stirring memories of climbs and ski trips past. Of friendships forged or tempered. Of blue skies and hot sun. Of impenetrable whiteouts and blowing snow. Of moments of desire and moments of release.

Fred was full of questions, most of which I couldn't answer. I love these mountains, and I have returned to them time and time again, but I am still only a visitor and don't know the heart and soul of them the way climbers who live in the region do.

Mostly I know isolated bits and pieces of them. The amazing bouldering on the petrified coral reef that overhangs Grassi Lake. The ice

LEFT: *Not for nothing has elegant Mount Assiniboine been dubbed the "Matterhorn of the Rockies". It is seen here from the north-east near the shore of Magog Lake. The famous North Ridge rises in the centre of the photograph.*

that adorns the walls and hangs in the gullies above the major roads. The continent-splitting summits and ridges of the Columbia Icefield peaks – and the uncertainty of trying to find our way around that icefield in a four-day whiteout. The camaraderie of nights in the clubhouse of the Alpine Club of Canada (and the uncertainty of trying to find that clubhouse after an evening in the bars of Canmore). The frustration of watching all two weeks of a vacation dissolve in endless rain. The pain of a telephone call telling me that a friend who has gone to the Rockies will never be coming back. The unforgettable afternoon spent sitting on the summit of Mount Castleguard, watching as a winter storm cleared from the stunning grandeur of the 2,000-meter (650-foot) north face of Mount Bryce.

I could tell him about some of these things, and it would be easy to take another day and drive him to places where he could enjoy Kodak Moments, but there were better things for him to take back to Texas than pictures of Mount

ABOVE: *Keeping well back from the fragile cornice, Bill March approaches the summit of Assiniboine. This is the final easy-angled section of the North Ridge, a magnificent alpine-style climb and deservedly a classic.*

To reach Berg Lake and the northern side of Mount Robson one makes an enjoyable 16-km (10-mile) hike from the roadhead in the Fraser Valley. Near the start lies beautiful Kinney Lake, its cold glacial waters reflecting distant Whitehorn Mountain. The trail takes the right-hand shoreline to enter the so-called Valley of a Thousand Falls beyond, initially over alluvial flats scattered with wild flowers.

Robson or the north face of Mount Kitchener taken from the highway. No, the best thing that I could give him to take back was the memory of more climbing. As we turned back toward Golden I said, "Since you seem to be done with that cough, how about some ice tomorrow?"

*   *   *

Lost again. Well, not lost, but misplaced. The walls of the gully had closed in, confining upward progress but offering no ice as far up as we could see. What had seemed obvious from the road was proving elusive in the forest. It wasn't that we couldn't find a trail – in fact it was the opposite. Others had been here before us, and there were well-defined tracks beaten in the snow – too many well-defined tracks, and we had obviously followed the wrong one.

"Guess we didn't traverse far enough."

"Either that or we traversed too far."

Down we went until the confining walls relaxed into the forest and we could contour leftward once again, ploughing our way slowly through deep snow until we turned a corner and halted, speechless, staring at the gossamer veil of blue-white ice hanging on the back wall of the narrow gully above.

Speechless? Not quite. I think I said something like "Holy shit!" and Fred managed to squeak, "We're going to climb *that*?"

Maybe he asked it rhetorically, or maybe it had just popped out reflexively, but for me the question was real, and thinking about it made me understand something about why I was there: not to climb this frozen cascade, but to find out if I *could* climb it. It was no steeper than I had managed a few days ago, but it went on and on, unrelentingly vertical for its whole length. And although the ramparts above were glowing in the morning light, the gully faced north and I knew that the ice would be both hard and brittle.

But so beautiful. Glowing in the light that reflected down from above.

An hour later, the steepness and difficulty parts of the question had been resolved. I had been able to climb 45 meters (148 feet) of vertical, sometimes fragile ice, and all that remained between me and a safe, comfortable belay stance was 10 meters (33 feet) of much easier ground.

"How much rope is left?"

"About fifteen feet." Fred is American and hadn't got the hang of meters and liters yet.

What to do? Although the ice was fracture-prone I could probably find solid placements for a couple of ice screws and belay safely from where I was, but why hang from my harness, in sub-freezing shade, on vertical ice, when there was a pair of stout pines growing out of the gully wall, in the sunshine, just a couple of minutes above me?

"There's a good belay spot just a bit out of reach. I'm going to head for it and when the rope comes tight, you just start climbing, okay? The first moves aren't all that steep."

So we simul-climbed the last bit, me going slowly on the last few stretches of easy ground to give him time to deal with the first moves below, until a final step brought me simultaneously into the sunshine and within reach of the trees. I tied off and put Fred on belay, forcing myself to double-check each step of these routine tasks, knowing that after the physical and emotional working over I had just received it would be all too easy to make a terminal mistake if I let myself go onto autopilot.

Satisfied with the security of the system, I called out the "On belay" to Fred, then leaned back, letting the tree trunks take my weight, and gradually let myself return from wherever it is that you go when the difficulty and danger of serious climbing take you out of the here-and-now.

Sensations first. The warmth of the sun and the astringent fragrance of the conifers. I took off my gloves and unzipped the top of my suit. (Had I been cold while I was climbing? I must have been, but I had no memory of it.)

Then colors. The red and purple of the ropes running down and then out of sight over the lip. The warm reddish-brown of the trees' bark and dense, dark green of their needles. The intense white of the snow, the golden tan of the rock, and the rich, glowing blue of the ice where the sun struck it.

And finally the silent splendor of the world around me. The sun pouring into this open spot in the gully turned it into a cosy haven, from which I could look across a forested valley to a long, snowy ridge that curved upward and buttressed an elegant, pyramidal peak. Huge, but so architecturally perfect that I was aware not of its size but only of its grace and symmetry. And behind that, as far into the distance as I could see were only ridge and wall, peak and spire, piercing the perfect blue of the sky.

*   *   *

Back in the Rockies. What more could anyone ask?

Bill March, one of the most renowned ice-climbers of the 1970s, climbs a bulging serac in the small but challenging Bugaboo Icefall. He is using aid but doubtless it would go clean with modern gear and techniques.

THE CANADIAN ROCKIES – FACTFILE

BACKGROUND

Extending some 1,600km (1,000 miles) from the US frontier almost to the Yukon, the myriad mountains of the Canadian Rockies form a narrow range separating the Great Plains of Alberta from the tangled Interior Ranges of British Columbia. More than 750 peaks top 2,750m (9,000ft) though the highest tend to be concentrated along the Continental Divide just west of the Icefields Parkway. These are steep and dramatic mountains of limestone and shale, heavily glaciated, cradling beautiful lakes and rising from thick coniferous forest, the haunt of moose, wolf and grizzly bear. A popular tourist venue in summer, the Rockies hold many winter ski resorts.

There are several fine mountain groups among the Interior Ranges of British Columbia immediately west of the Rockies, but most renowned is the Bugaboos, a cluster of spectacular granite spires rising from an icefield in the Purcell Range that lies parallel to and only 48km (30 miles) west of the Rockies crest.

The first climbers followed the Canadian Pacific Railway when it finally broached the Selkirks – one of the Interior Ranges – in 1885 and built a hotel at hitherto inaccessible Rogers Pass, close below the sharp pyramid of Mount Sir Donald. The ascent of this peak in 1890 and other Selkirk summits by British and American alpinists laid the foundations of mountaineering as a sport in North America.

By the turn of the century emphasis was turning to the Rockies themselves, also made accessible by the CPR, who developed a climbing centre at Lake Louise and brought over professional alpine guides. Most notable was the redoubtable Austrian Conrad Kain, who made the first ascents of Robson, Bugaboo Spire and many other important peaks in the years before and during World War I.

ACCESS

Although close to the cities of Calgary and Edmonton and pierced by three major railways and several important roads,

once off the beaten track this is real wilderness country. The towns of Banff and Jasper lie at either end of this most important section of the Rockies, with the spectacular 240-km (150-mile) Icefields Parkway linking the two and giving some form of access to the eastern side of the range. National Parks encompass the entire Alberta flank of the divide, and various Provincial Parks, much of the British Columbia flank, while the Bugaboos are protected as an Alpine Recreation Area. Camping

Mount Robson	*12,972ft / 3,954m*
Mount Assiniboine	*11,870ft / 3,618m*
Mount Temple	*11,626ft / 3,544m*
Mount Bryce	*11,507ft / 3,507m*
Mount Athabasca	*11,452ft / 3,491m*
Mount Kitchener	*11,400ft / 3,475m*
North Howser Tower	*11,150ft / 3,399m*
Mount Edith Cavell	*11,033ft / 3,363m*
Bugaboo Spire	*10,420ft / 3,176m*
Pigeon Spire	*10,250ft / 3,124m*
Mount Castleguard	*10,100ft / 3,078m*
Snowpatch Spire	*10,050ft / 3,063m*

is controlled, and climbers and overnight hikers are required to register at national park offices, though less strict regulations apply elsewhere.

HIKING AND CLIMBING

Not really a hiking area, the Bugaboos offer some of the finest alpine rockclimbing on the continent and a guardianed climbing hut enables many routes to be completed in a day. In winter the Bugaboo Glacier is a major heli-skiing venue.

In the Rockies themselves long backpacking trips demand serious wilderness skills but there are many short hiking trails close to the main tourist areas. Alpine-style climbing on large mountains ranges from straightforward snow-climbs around to daunting north-face routes on treacherous ice and poor rock, while there is an abundance of pure rockclimbing of all grades and lengths. Long frozen waterfalls provide winter sport and back-country skiing is popular. There are a number of climbing huts and bivouac shelters but otherwise backpacking to a camp at the foot of the mountain is usual.

Bill March sets off down the short summit crest of Mount Robson. Huge cornices curl to the left while steep ice falls away on the right. It was early morning when the picture was taken and the weather looked unsettled. We had to be sure to locate our ascent line before starting to descend the steep slopes of the Roof.

The Land of Red Rocks

South-western USA

STEVE ROPER

"The sun struck our dome with startling suddenness, and the sandstone, cheerless red in the pre-dawn, exploded into crimson that seemed to have infinite depth. We felt we could get up and walk straight into the interior of the rock, maybe the interior of the earth itself. Once again, this was unnerving, as if our familiar world had become Triassic overnight."

The Watchman is a small mountain and rises only 2,500ft (760m) above the Virgin River in Utah's Zion National Park, but its form is as fine as any alpine peak. Here the mountain is seen from the north over the North Fork of the river during spring spate.

From my cramped window seat, looking down 33,000 feet (10,000 meters) onto North America's mountainous south-western desert, I recalled the story of an English travel writer who, around 1895, had scorned this vast "wasteland". In a dusty café, grumpy after a fatiguing day's ride in a stagecoach, he was offered the local delicacy, roasted sage grouse. He refused haughtily, exclaiming, "Damn anything with wings that will stay in such country!" My jet, its wings glinting in the too-bright troposphere, heeded this advice with a vengeance, and in an hour I looked down upon the more hospitable-looking farmlands and river cities of the Midwest. Not many people appreciate the South-west at first glance, and many years ago I was no exception. In this 200,000-square-mile (518,000 square-kilometer) region (I am talking mainly about northern Arizona and southern Utah) vast tracts of land are flat, seemingly lifeless and, quite frankly, boring. Sometimes you can drive for hours seeing only sagebrush and creosote bushes. Sandstorms swirl out of nowhere, and I have had windshields permanently pitted by grains of sand that would have scalped me, had I been outside. I've fried in summer heat, learned what "chilled to the bone" means during April cold snaps.

It took many trips, over fifteen years, before I came to utter those words of finality: "You know, I wouldn't mind living out here." Now, as I approach middle age, I dream of leaving the big city behind forever and striding from my little adobe cabin at dawn and wandering into a new canyon, or through a solitary grove of aspens, or across crimson-orange slabs so smooth that they have been given an official name: slickrock. There is so much to see in the South-west – if you know how to look. John Cleare's images show that he knows how to look, but, of course, they are photographs, and not recorded is one of the most telling characteristics of the South-west: the silence. One could argue that mountains are silent, too, but so often they have a burbling stream, the wind coursing over a ridge, tremolos of thunder, the creak of a glacier, an avalanche or rockfall far in the distance. The canyon country of the South-west is the most silent place I've ever been.

My wife and I were once staying in the campground in Zion National Park, as captivated as ever with the orange and tan cliffs, stained with black water streaks, all contrasting beautifully against the deepest blue sky imaginable. But Zion had not been quiet, and, with murmurs of a hundred

campers and belchings of a dozen tour buses in my ears, I had suggested a visit to the remote canyons of south-central Utah. Here, I knew, were the sounds of silence. Still, I was not prepared for what we "heard".

Words cannot convey silence any more than photographs, so I should stop right here and talk my publisher into leaving a blank page of glaring nothingness. For this is what it seemed like that night as we slept tentless under a rounded dome, 40 miles (64 kilometers) from the nearest village and paved road, under stars close enough to pluck. It was blank. White. Or was it black? The silence was a presence, a presence of nothingness. The silence of death? We began to get uneasy, to wish for a plane overhead, or for the rumble of a faraway thunderstorm. But nothing. Gradually, we began to appreciate the quiet for what it was: not scary, just unique.

The sun struck our dome with startling suddenness, and the sandstone, cheerless red in the pre-dawn, exploded into crimson that seemed to have infinite depth. We felt we could get up and walk straight into the interior of the rock, maybe the interior of the earth itself. Once again, this was unnerving, as if our familiar world had become Triassic overnight.

What came after that apocalyptic dawn was less mystical, less silent, but more typical of a day exploring in the South-west. The canyons near the junction of the Colorado and Escalante rivers are not well known to tourists, though hardy adventurers have known about them for sixty years or more. No official trails

BELOW LEFT: The Grand Canyon, a place of great cliffs, sharp peaklets and huge voids. This picture, from the South Rim's Pima Point, looks north-east over the Colorado River nearly 4,500ft (1,370m) below towards the pyramid-crowned mesas on the left known as Isis Temple and Buddha Temple.

BELOW RIGHT: Sonoran Desert, Arizona: the Eagletail Mountains are seen at mid-winter sun-up lining the southern horizon of the Harqualaha Plain. The "Feathers" pinnacles can just be made out on the highest summit. A giant saguaro cactus provides a typical foreground.

The renowned sandstone towers of Totem Pole and Yei Be Chei stand in the Navajo Tribal Park of Monument Valley, the most spectacular formations of a dramatic landscape beloved of film-makers. Needless to say, these towers have been climbed. Totem Pole also featured in Clint Eastwood's thriller movie The Eiger Sanction.

RIGHT: *Hardly a mountain but certainly mountainous – one of the bizarre pinnacles that adorn the Grand Canyon. This one is called "Duck on Rock" and stands on the South Rim near Shoshone Point. The prominent pyramid of "Vishnu Temple" rises in the distance.*

exist, and few road signs tell you where you are. You must get out a good map and stride off on your own, with no footprints to follow in the more remote canyons. At first you'll wonder if you've started in the right place, for no sign of a canyon is visible. We felt immediately that uncertain feeling which shows you're off on yet another adventure.

Working our way down a gentle sandy wash, curving with the contours of the land, we realized after a quarter of a mile that, yes, we had entered a canyon, if by "canyon" one means a trench 5 feet deep and 5 feet wide (1.5 by 1.5 meters). The width stayed the same as we progressed, but ever so subtly the height of the walls increased. The sunlight vanished. Soon we were in yet another place that has had to be defined by a modern phrase: a slot canyon.

As we progressed farther down the slot, evidence of flash floods, the phenomenon that had created these amazing trenches, took on a surreal aspect, for we saw skinned logs as thick as a person wedged 30 feet (10 meters) above our heads. The first time I saw this bizarre sight, I thought a tree on the rim above had died, fallen, and ended up perched picturesquely inside the gorge. I soon realized my stupidity, for there were no trees of that size growing within 3 miles (5 kilometers) of us. Someday I'd like to sit atop a slot canyon during a flash flood and look down into the action. You don't need silence all the time.

Soon we came to a widening of the canyon, and here cottonwoods, their leaves radiant gold in the autumn, appeared in the distance. It might seem redundant to see golden leaves against a background of burnt-orange sandstone cliffs, but the colors complemented each other magically. As we rounded a gentle corner, a great horned owl burst forth from a shadowy hole in the cliff and disappeared around the next bend. We followed it for a full hour. These are not sights I saw from my airplane window.

The Grand Canyon, however, is visible for a full ten minutes on the flight east from LA to New York: a vast, terraced landscape totally unintelligible from such an immense height. This place, seen at ground level, is as different from a slot canyon as Greece is from Denmark. I must say that I have a love-hate relationship with this world-famous canyon. The views from the traditional turnouts on the two rims have always been disappointing to me, mainly because I'm rarely there at dawn or dusk, times when the oblique lighting casts mile-long shadows against cliffs and buttes that radiate all shades of red and ochre and brown. Only by dropping down inside this huge gash in the earth can you begin to make sense of its size. I have been lucky enough to take four such trips, each lasting more than a week. Trails are rare here, and my trips have avoided them for the most part. Cross-country travel is neither easy nor recommended for most hikers, and I, who call myself highly experienced on off-trail terrain, have found the walking to be the toughest I've ever done. Bad footing, extreme temperatures, carnivorous cacti, cliffs to be descended, avoided, or climbed – there's always something to make you tired.

So why go? Here the lure is neither colors nor silence, and not even the incomprehensible scale, which, after all, is ... incomprehensible. No, what you live for down in the bowels of the earth are the special moments of beauty that come upon you so suddenly you are speechless. It can be a dead agave cactus, its golden tan leaves crackling in the breeze. It can be a small cottonwood tucked away in an alcove, or a canyon wren whistling a descending song so winsome as to make you imitate its melody. Often, the magical moment of the day comes at the very end, when, thirsty and staggering under a 50-pound (23-kilogram) pack, you finally arrive in the area where you thought you might camp and, yes, there is water, life-giving water! This might be a tiny stream; it could be a tiny but deep pool where rainwater has collected; sometimes it is a mere seep in a canyon wall that shines with chartreuse moss.

The South-west isn't all stark nature, of course. There are towns scattered about, and many highways crisscross the region. This is also the land of cowboys and Indians. During the late nineteenth century our expansionist and racist forebears ravaged the native peoples, killing them, betraying them, and spreading diseases such as smallpox and cholera. It is not a sterling chapter in the history of the United States. The Native Americans who survived were shunted off to reservations in places thought worthless, one of which was the South-west. One fairly peaceful tribe, the Navajo, didn't have to go far: they already lived nearby. Today they occupy an enormous chunk of north-eastern Arizona and anyone who travels through here will have ambivalent feelings. Poverty reigns, alcoholism abounds, and the Navajo's age-old culture is disappearing rapidly. Yet one senses that the people still have ties to the land that we non-natives can only envy. Notice the doorways to the hogans, their tiny dwelling places: they invariably face east, toward the rising sun. Note the proud, serene look on the faces of the elders: they

These tantalising pinnacles stand off the south-western corner of Rain God Mesa, another of the shapely sandstone features in Monument Valley.

seem to know their place in the spiritual world, and they don't need ministers or priests to tell them this.

The Navajos proudly own and administer one of the most dramatic landscapes on the planet – Monument Valley, on the Utah-Arizona border. Every moviegoer has surely seen brave white cowboys pursuing hapless red men through sandy washes with enormous sandstone towers looming in the background. One almost expects war whoops, the crackling of rifles, the hoofbeats of horses. Every time I go to this splendid place, I think of John Wayne and the United States Cavalry.

Although the towers of Monument Valley are emblematic of the South-west, they cannot really be called "mountains". But the region has plenty of high peaks and remote ranges, including Utah's Henry Mountains, the last-named range in the contiguous United States. This 12,000-foot-high (3,500-meter) chain, out in the middle of nowhere, wasn't fully explored until the 1920s, and even today its summits see few footprints. Standing atop such remote ranges, you gaze out in every direction without seeing a single man-made object. Adventurers who like to hike or climb without crowds should be ecstatic here.

Other ranges are far more accessible, and a few towns, like Moab, Utah, have the best of all worlds: 12,000-foot (3,500-meter) peaks half-an-hour distant, the

Dusk over remote Spanish Bottom at the head of the Colorado River's Cataract Canyon. Rusty Baillie and I camped here to explore the nearby Maze and Land of Standing Rocks before continuing with our white-water descent of the Canyon.

Colorado River, largest in the South-west, on the town's outskirts, and psychedelic desert scenery fifteen minutes from town. In summer you play in the cool, aspen-covered hills; in winter you traipse through nameless red-rock canyons or take a raft trip down the Colorado. Moab is not a pretty town, yet its location in a fertile valley next to the Colorado is almost unmatchable. Two national parks lie within easy reach, and if you had to choose a base of operations for your South-west experience, this is the place.

Arches National Park, a ten-minute drive north of town, is a hodgepodge of cliffs, towers, and, as the name implies, arches. And what fabulous arches! The geologic story is complex, but, in essence, tectonic forces uplifted the land, water seeped into fault lines, ice and erosion expanded these narrow cracks, and, over millions of years, the elements created great trenches and corresponding fins of harder rock. Then these narrow fins began to erode, with weaker rock breaking off in chunks. Often, when an entire section of fin collapsed, an isolated tower

We found this natural arch somewhere in the bewildering Maze canyon system. The picture is taken looking out from the all but inaccessible cave beneath it, wherein we found flakes of chipped stone, which set us wondering ...

would remain. If a mere pinhole appeared in a fin, then the wind became the primary sculptor – Nature's Michelangelo. If the hole became large enough, then, *voilà*!, an arch was born. Because of its unique "finned" geology, this rather small region contains more arches than anywhere else in the world – some 1,500 have been catalogued. I am embarrassed to say that I have seen only about fifty of these arches during the course of probably fifteen days of hiking. Two, I always return to, like a salmon to its river of birth. Landscape Arch, its span the world's longest, is so thin and fragile that I have always been too timid to walk across it, knowing that one day, tomorrow? forty years hence?, it will collapse, probably with an arrogant climber aboard it. Delicate Arch, an exquisite formation standing alone on sloping acres of orange-red slickrock, is so beautiful and so famous that the Utah car license plate bears its image. Go there at dawn and you'll never forget it.

An hour's drive south of Moab will bring you to Canyonlands National Park, an enormous region whose most salient feature is its complexity. Towers, buttes, arches, and fins abound, and connecting these are labyrinths of corridors and canyons. This 500-square-mile (1,300-square-kilometer) jumble of cliff, desert, and canyon might still be unexplored had the great uranium boom of the 1950s not taken place. But we needed this element for the Cold War, and hundreds of miners, many working alone, fanned out in Jeeps and on horseback. It was like a second Gold Rush for a few years, but luckily not much uranium was found. Jeep tracks in fragile desert soil last a long time, however, and the slightly scarred landscape will be with us for the foreseeable future. Even with these signs of man, it would be very easy to get lost here, and several place names reflect this: the Labyrinth, Lost Canyon, Meander Canyon, and the Maze. This latter place, perfectly named, has been described as "one of the most remote and inaccessible sections" of the lower forty-eight states. I hope to go there some day.

Whenever I pass by the cliffs of Canyonlands or the towers of Monument Valley, I am reminded that I was once a rockclimber. I still look for possible new routes, though I don't think I'll be trying many of them. I had many wonderful moments hanging around on the rocks, but some of the bad times are as vivid as last night's nightmares. I recall my hands being bloodied in hideous jamcracks; I still feel the blisters coming on as I trudged across miles of sand and cacti to reach a crumbling, unnamed hunk of blazing stone. Once, after rappelling 700 feet (200 meters) down the side of a vertical tower in a rainstorm and so covered in liquid red sandstone as to look like Thomas Hardy's famous reddleman, I happened to glance at the carabiners I'd used for rappelling. I gagged, for they had been sliced one-third of the way through by the abrasive combination of moving rope and wet sand. Another few rappels and I wouldn't now be telling this story.

My most petrifying climbing experience in the South-west took place in 1962, when I was barely old enough to vote, let alone possess judgment. I badly wanted to climb a spire called Cleopatra's Needle, an awesome formation 225 feet (70 meters) high, thin as a knifeblade. This freakish pinnacle had been ascended only once, six years earlier. A few sentences in the first-ascent account had both scared and intrigued me: "The second man had no problems taking pitons out. Few of the thirty even needed pounding with a hammer." Surely this wasn't true! I was traveling with a non-climbing girlfriend that autumn, and we zigzagged through the region, hiking and doing things young lovers do. I had brought climbing equipment, thinking I could teach Sharon if necessary.

She was a brave lass and on Cleo I easily dragged her up to a belay ledge 100 feet (30 meters) above the ground. She stared up at the next section, a dead-vertical wall 125-feet (40-meters) high, soft as cheddar, and split by a single thin crack, through which we could see daylight – the other side of the spire. She rebelled. I too wanted no part of it. But I was brimming with a dangerous drug, testosterone, and so, after teaching Sharon the rudiments of belaying and promising glibly that I wouldn't fall and that she needn't go to the summit, I set off, pounding pitons into the buttery sandstone with blows Thor would have been proud of. This was classic artificial climbing: a piton every few feet. On granite, it would have been a dream, but here the pitons kept shifting under my weight, and a few lower ones rattled out as I progressed. After two hours of this I was scared witless and covered in red dust and sweat,

The rock architecture in the Maze is incredible and – if you are adept on fragile sandstone – the climbing potential could be exciting! Caused by aeons of water seepage, the colours on this arcing wall reflect the atmosphere of this landscape.

The giant saguaro cactus (Carnegiea gigantea) is the characteristic plant in much of the south-western desert country and even appears as the emblem on Arizona license plates. The plants can grow 30–40ft (10–12m) tall and provide homes for a wide variety of creatures, from owls to snakes.

wondering why Sharon and I weren't instead cavorting naked in a motel room. If a piton popped while I was perched on it, I wouldn't have to worry about my questionable belayer holding me: I would zipper every piton, smash down onto Sharon's ledge, and end up the size of Tiny Tim. As happens near the top of all artificial pitches, or so it seems, I began to run out of the correct size of pitons, hammering big ones part way into narrow cracks and tapping little pitons until they almost disappeared into wider cracks. Just as I was ready to self-destruct from panic, I pulled up onto the minuscule summit to see the rotting rappel slings left by the first-ascent party. Somehow I got down alive (cleaning many of the pitons with my hands) and found Sharon weeping from fear, rage, and relief. I promised her we wouldn't do any more climbing, and we didn't for a full week.

After a decade of such nonsense, I soon began listening more closely to the words of the famous desert climber Chuck Pratt: "To gain any lasting worth from what the desert has to offer, we had to learn to put our pitons and ropes away and to go exploring in silence, keeping our eyes very open. It wasn't easy. We wasted a lot of time climbing until we got the knack." And, sure enough, once I had discarded the rope I felt much more positive about the region.

Fresh in my memory now is neither a death rappel nor a shifting piton but rather a short trip that combined many elements of what I most love about the mountains of the South-west. My friend Dave Cook and I had thought about hiking and climbing in the remote Eagle Tail Range, not far west of Phoenix. We loved the name, yet knew nothing about the place. An adventure in the making! Fate, in the form of a missed connection, conspired against us, and we had a mere day and a half left – not enough time for the Eagle Tails. Quickly looking at a map, our fingers simultaneously pointed to one of the more famous small ranges in North America: the Superstitions. Childlike visions of discovering the fabled Lost Dutchman Mine flashed through our heads. The rumors began 130 years ago: a cranky old miner was secretly transporting great chunks of gold out of the range. People died or disappeared trying to find his supposed mine, and then the Dutchman died. More rumors sprang up: there was a map and maybe it was his. Maybe the cryptic marks on this map of dubious provenance could be decoded. Incredibly, adventurers still comb the mountains for the lost riches. And we would be among them, though of course we just wanted an excuse to get out into the hills.

I regard the trailhead on the southern edge of the Superstitions as Nirvana. This is because I love sharp peaks, cactus, and birds, and here the combination is splendid. Most prominent of the ten or fifteen varieties of South-west cacti that grow here in profusion is that emblem of Arizona: the saguaro. This huge ribbed plant, with its multiple "arms," is one of the strangest desert sights. Elf owls and gila woodpeckers nest inside these plants – you will hear the latter bird upon closing your car door. Roadrunners and curve-billed thrashers scuttle about, and hawks soar overhead.

RIGHT: Three pinnacles form the triple summits – or "Feathers" – set along the exposed crest of Eagle Tail Peak in Arizona's Sonoran Desert. Here Rusty Baillie bombs the strenuous crack leading to the top of the highest Feather. It is New Year's Day, an ideal time for such desert climbing.

We began walking up a gentle trail, with wildflowers visible everywhere. Within minutes we saw a sight I'd never seen and have never seen again. This was the fearsome-looking Gila monster, the largest lizard of the Americas. Eighteen inches (46 centimeters) long, beaded with red and yellow, it stared at us with primordial eyes. We knew it was venomous but also how sluggish it was. We three regarded each other solemnly for a few minutes, then Dave and I headed uphill to a pass overlooking our real goal – not the Lost Dutchman Mine, but Weaver's Needle, a mountainous spire looming a mile ahead. The ascent of this tower was mostly non-technical and went smoothly, and we descended in the late-afternoon sunlight whooping like Indians.

Soon it was dusk, but we weren't worried, for we had carried sleeping bags and wine, the two essential ingredients. Shortly we discovered a rocky shelf with a vista far out to the north. Here, in the moonlight, we sat and talked for hours about the Dutchman, riches, monsters, saguaros, canyons, emptiness. Finally, as midnight approached, we both became aware of the utter silence. It was time to stop talking, listen to the nothingness, and get a few hours of sleep before facing the next day and the adventures that were sure to come.

Rusty Baillie in action on one of the steep and delicate walls at Granite Dells, an excellent small climbing area outside Prescott in Arizona. A much larger area close by, Granite Mountain has developed into a major climbing venue thanks to Baillie and his students at Prescott College.

SOUTH-WESTERN USA – FACTFILE

BACKGROUND

Unique in this book, South-western USA is a large area of essentially high desert country, scattered with small mountain ranges and strange mountainous outcroppings. Although the land surface is predominately sandstone, in places weathered into spectacular formations, there are many areas of volcanic intrusion or exposure.

The major feature of the region is the great Colorado River, which on its journey from the Rockies to the Sea of Cortez, traverses a series of dramatic canyons first explored by the one-armed Civil War hero John Wesley Powell in 1869. Much of the desert country remained uncharted until the uranium boom of the early 1950s. Shiprock was first climbed in 1939 and serious desert climbing started only in 1956.

ACCESS

Federal Lands cover large areas of Arizona, Utah and the Four Corners country. These include everything from national parks and Bureau of Land Management Reserves to Indian Lands and Military Reservations. In national parks entrance fees are usually charged, Back Country Permits are required for camping and bivouacking, while specific hiking routes and climbing may be controlled.

Shiprock, Spider Rock, the Totem Pole, and certain other spectacular rock features on Indian Lands – notably on Navajo territory – are strictly forbidden to climbers.

Distances in the region are great. The main highway network is excellent but some approaches may be on dirt roads that are impassable immediately after heavy rain. Wheeled vehicles are prohibited off-road in many federal areas, and long hikes are often necessary to reach scenic or climbing locations.

Summer here is hot, making spring and autumn the prime climbing/hiking seasons, although adequate water should always be carried. Winter, too, can offer good hiking when snowfall on the higher ground between December and March renders this landscape particularly attractive.

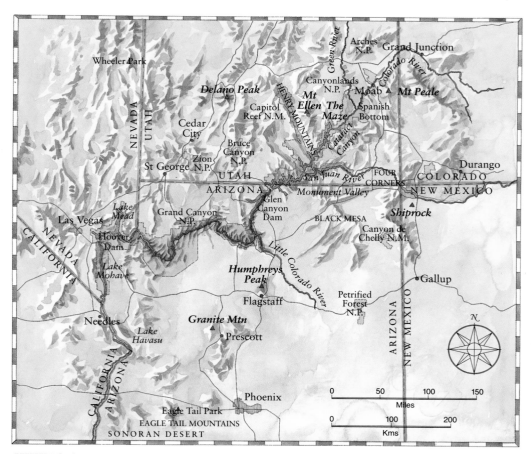

HIKING AND CLIMBING

Hiking possibilities here are endless, up mountains, down canyons and always through exciting scenery. However, any route off the beaten track must be treated seriously – this is big, remote country with heat, flash floods and rattlesnakes among the potential hazards. For beginners, an introduction to the area on one of the popular trails in perhaps the Grand Canyon or Zion might be advisable before multi-day trips into remote areas are attempted.

Obviously the dramatic sandstone features attract the climber, but the rock here is poor, the situations serious and the techniques specialised. The granite areas are more accommodating, the Eagle Tails offering good potential, while places like Granite Mountain near Prescott are well developed with hundreds of guide-booked climbs.

La Salle Mountains:	
Mount Peale	*12,721ft / 3,877m*
Henry Mountains:	
Mount Ellen	*11,615ft / 3,540m*
Zion National Park:	
Great White Throne	*6,744ft / 2,056m*
The Watchman	*6,555ft / 1,998m*
Monument Valley Tribal Park:	
Totem Pole	*300ft / 100m*
Fisher Towers group:	
Castleton Tower	*6,656ft / 2,029m*
The Titan	*5,600ft / 1,707m*
Granite Mountain	*7,700ft / 2,347m*
Shiprock	*7,178ft / 2,188m*
Eagle Tail Peak	*3,304ft / 1,007m*
Spider Rock	*800ft / 250m*

The Unpredictable Mountains

Patagonia

JOHN CLEARE

*"Behind us spread a moonscape where the enormous crevasse-wrinkled
glacier swept down from the ice-cap where horizon and cloud blended
as one. Ahead was a different world. Slopes fell away to a sunlit
valley lined by a wall of craggy snow-streaked peaks. An azure
lake surrounded by green forest glinted in the sun.
If ever a valley beckoned, it was this one."*

The wind was fierce. It came in great gusts. I could only flatten myself against the shattered rock of the ridge crest and hang on until the blast had died. This was no place to stumble, for the holds were loose and the exposure awesome. We should have roped up, but strung out along the arête as we were the rope would have been a live thing – unhandleable – more a hazard than a safeguard on what surely was only a scramble. The crest rose slightly and flattened to a slabby boss. Ahead broken rock fell steeply away and a few stones piled in a token cairn indicated the summit. Crouching around it we shouted congratulations at each other, only for the useless words to be swept away into space by the gale. This was Cerro Almirante Nieto – a mouthful of a mountain, but a worthy Patagonian summit. I'd made it – at last.

I had hoped to come here thirty years ago. The incredible granite spires of the Paine had been the talk of the climbing world when I was invited to join some friends in an attempt on the Fortress. But my business partners were unhappy about my prospective absence and career came first. So, my friends climbed the Fortress while I photographed the new London Bridge. Big deal. The Falklands Conflict in 1983, between Britain and Argentina, scuppered any subsequent plans but not before the renowned American climber Royal Robbins advised me not to visit Patagonia expecting to climb.

"The climbing would be tremendous," he explained, "if the weather weren't so goddamn miserable. Up high the storms last for ever. Nope, if it's climbing you want, stay in California where the sun shines. But go there to hike, go to take photographs – the landscape's as stunning as anywhere in the world."

Eventually, another opportunity arrived and, with several friends, I planned to

Our party traverses back from the summit along the shattered crest of Cerro Almirante Nieto, the picture giving little idea of the fierce wind that threatened to sweep us into space. Lago Torres lies far below on the left, while beyond the Rio Paine and Lago Azul tawny foothills stretch towards the distant pampas of Argentina.

This is the south-west view from the summit of Cerro Almirante Nieto. We look in the opposite direction to the previous picture. Here the view is past the southern ridges of Los Cuernos ("the Horns") to the lake country south of the Paine massif. Lago Nordenskjold lies below; Lago Peho, beyond; and, in the far distance, the head of the torturous Ultima Esperanza fjord – the sea.

visit the two most famous Patagonian mountain groups – Fitzroy in Argentina and the Paine in Chile. Mindful of Royal's warning we decided that our first attempt should be to trek around each massif before homing in for a swift stab at one of the less difficult peaks. Both circumnavigations, while fairly ambitious, would provide good introductions to the area. They ought to be feasible whatever the weather, and if perchance the elements did prevent the subsequent climb – too bad, at least we'd not have wasted days on a fruitless siege. The circuit of the Paine alone, I learned, usually took at least a week; our airline schedule allowed us the bare minimum of eight days.

Then I discovered that the eastern segment of the Paine Circuit was tame and comparatively uninteresting. If we could avoid it by crossing the main Paine crest into the blind valley of the Rio Ascensio in the heart of the massif, we could not only climb Cerro Almirante Nieto, a worthy objective apparently not particularly difficult, but also visit the renowned Towers of Paine close by.

Al Stevenson regards the strangely malevolent snout of the huge Ventisquero Grey as it calves into Lago Grey. This is an eerie place, especially in the sullen weather that we encountered. The lake surface is only some 150ft (50m) above sea level, and the glacier at this point is actually 2½ miles (4km) wide. However, it is split by the forested rognon on the left, so less than a third of the snout can be seen.

But I could find no record of a pass and I was actually told that a crossing was not feasible without roped climbing – although photographs I'd seen suggested otherwise. Anyway, we decided it was worth a try.

I feared that it might be a bad omen starting a mountain journey with sea-sickness. Daniel, our local contact, had arranged for us to cross Lago Pehoe in a small fishing smack, a good move that saved a first day's walk from the Ranger Station. It was a source of wonder to me how such a vessel had reached such a lake. As the boat chugged down-channel we were treated to that famous view of the Cordillera Paine from the south, the bizarre turrets of Los Cuernos ("the Horns") glowing gold in the evening sun while Cerro Almirante Nieto and Paine Grande sulked under dark cloud-caps.

But once out of shelter we might have been in Drake Passage: short, steep

waves crashed against the boat, horizontal hail lashed the deck and we scrambled below hatches to imbibe excellent Chilean wine while it was still available. A mistake. Eight unhappy sailors stumbled on land in the dark, to erect their tents on a rainswept shore.

It was an unlikely introduction to unique mountains.

Our route lay initially up the west flank of the massif before crossing a high pass into the valley system that separates it on the north from the Heilo Sur – the Patagonian ice-cap. For a day we tramped along the shores of Lago Grey on a well-worn trail in a steady, almost freezing downpour. All was grey – the water, the sky and the clouds that occasionally parted long enough for a glimpse of new snow on the craggy flanks of Paine Grande. Had we not been true Brits, nurtured on rainswept mountains, our morale would probably also have been grey. Was there a pioneering Señor Grey, I asked myself, or was the name merely a caustic comment on the prevailing weather?

Open woods gave way to tall rainforest of Magellanic beech, the stately evergreens characteristic of these southern climes. We camped on a rocky shore close by a decrepit hut and watched odd icebergs cruise down the lake. Though the rain held off, the following morning was dreary and threatening when we scrambled down to the imposing snout of the Ventisquero Grey, the huge Grey Glacier, the source of the icebergs. In the dull light and devoid of all colour it seemed strangely malevolent, a lifeless place of primeval cold and damp. Above the glacier our now vestigial trail continued along steep forest-clad slopes where we waded through knee-deep greenery below the great trees, frequently stepping round or over fallen trunks. And again we camped, this time on small earthy ledges buttressed with gnarled roots beneath the dark canopy.

"... drifted snow and naked boulders – Felt free air astir to windward – Knew I'd stumbled on the Pass." Kipling's description could well fit the Passo Paine. A steep climb of some 2,500 feet (760 metres) through the brooding forest, a fight through vertical thickets of dwarf beech and then over scree and snow patches, led eventually to a wide saddle. Behind us spread a moonscape in which the enormous crevasse-wrinkled glacier swept down from the ice-cap where horizon and cloud blended as one. Ahead was a different world. Slopes fell away to a sunlit valley lined by a wall of craggy snow-streaked peaks. An azure lake surrounded by green forest glinted in the sun. If ever a valley beckoned, it was this one.

But it was not as easy as it looked. We strode gaily down sun-warmed scree and leaped mossy rills to enter the zone of dwarf beech. The tangled bushes grew in trackless, glutinous bog so only after much frustrating effort did we finally reach the valley bottom, muddied but unbowed. Yellow daisies sprung in clumps among the stones beside the lively torrent in which we washed down our boots and gaiters before crossing on a convenient fallen log to find the lake. Daniel and Horacio started a brew going on the shore while the others stretched out in the sun to dry off. Scrambling around looking for photographs I watched several miniature icebergs drift serenely away from the snout of the small icefall that tumbled into the far side of the lake. I puzzled over how to reach the glacier above and wondered if any of the surrounding summits had names.

The Rio de los Perros – the "River of the Lost Ones" – that drains the lake is a large and powerful torrent. Horacio explained that the evocative name was given by a pioneering shepherd who lost his dogs in an attempt to cross, and I could well understand how. But then the ranching had failed, the national park had come and now there was a neat wire-and-log footbridge downstream from the lake. Down the trail we encountered a bedraggled group of Chilean students hiking in the opposite direction, their trendy leisure clothes and their over-stuffed

The moonscape of the Ventisquero Grey seen from near the upper limit of the beech forest below the Passo Paine. At its current state of retreat the glacier still extends some 12 miles (19km) from the ice cap. We were intrigued by the tempting rock needle on the right, which appears to reach about 6,000ft (1,800m), and is unnamed.

knapsacks hung with mugs and mattresses suggesting that they were as out of their depth as they were ill-equipped. Sure, they'd survive unless they hit a terrible storm on the pass, but would they learn from their experience? We could only wish them good luck. Progress? Perhaps.

It's a long 6 miles (10 kilometres) down the valley and round the bend to the shore of the next lake, the large Lago Dickson. Most of the way lies through primeval forest and as we were weary the going was heavy – the forest floor, lush with herbage and scattered with flowers, is littered with the fallen trunks and branches of centuries. I was glad we were on our way down rather than up the valley. Sometimes on knolls above the river there were clearings from where we could see above the tree-tops to the stark rock walls of Indian's Head, Shield and Trident glowing in the afternoon sun. Sooner or later we must find a way over that crest.

Lago Dickson stretches some 5 miles (8 kilometres) from its outflow where the Rio Paine is born to Ventisquero Dickson, the tortured arm of the ice-cap which calves into its northern extremity. I'd read that the ice is reckoned to have had

My companion Mike Parsons was already at the summit of the Passo Paine. I was eager to catch him up, so that I too could look down into the Los Perros valley beyond the lip. The cloud-capped mountain wall on the right is the northern extremity of the Paine Grande massif, with the main ridge crest of the Cordillera Paine itself extending beyond.

retreated some 5,000 feet (1,500 metres) up the lake over the past century. Now the great icefall dropped steeply from the plateau through a portal of craggy nunataks into the lake. A dramatic spectacle worth seeing close up, but there was no time for the three-day side trip. We were erecting our tents beside the lake shore when Daniel called us over to a low mound covered in daisies.

"P'raps ziz is Mister Dickson's House?" he suggested, and sure enough the mound covered what was left of a low tent-shaped log cabin. Nearby stood a clump of gooseberry bushes and the rotted remains of a fence crossing what had once been a meadow. But it was a beautiful place without the sad atmosphere of defeated dreams that so often pervades abandoned settlements.

Rainbows played between the showers as we set off again down the broad strath of the Rio Paine. It was attractive country, an overgrown meadowland of flowery tussocks, stands of low bushes and occasional ghostly coppices of skeletal tree trunks. On the well-used trail we met another gaggle of youthful hikers.

"Someone must have written up the Paine in a Santiago pop magazine," complained Fowler.

"It's long vacation at university – summer holidays, you see," explained Daniel.

"I could certainly sell 'em some proper gear," declared Mike, an outdoor equipment manufacturer. "South America's sure to be a great·new leisure market."

At every opportunity I examined the southern wall of the valley through my binoculars. Still high and snow-streaked, here it appeared much less formidable. The savage summits that had frowned down on Lago Dickson had given way to lower, more rounded mountains as we approached Lago Paine. It looked worth a try.

So we camped early, close above the western end of the lake. We'd surely earned the rest. A horseman came into camp leading a *burro*. It was the *gaucho* Daniel had hired to bring up fresh food and, at my request, Daniel asked him if he knew of a route crossing the ridge into the Ascensio glen.

A definitive "no" was the reply and the comment "... *muy intransitable*!" – very impassable – was followed by much waving of hands. But we ate steak that night and drank good red wine under the stars. Tomorrow would tell.

Up the hillside we went, with heavy rucksacks but a twinge of excitement, for this was new ground. For a "grassy slope" it was very steep. At first there were colourful flowers and odd bushes but once we had passed the prominent waterfall in its deep gulch the vegetation became sparser and more alpine. The view opened

BELOW: *A tussock of moss saxifrage (S. bryoides is its Latin name) provides a foreground to this view of the Rio Paine strath, as seen from high on the steep hillside heading for the anticipated but unknown pass over the divide. Cerro Ohnet rises over just-glimpsed Lago Dickson in the distance.*

RIGHT: *The world-renowned Torres del Paine rise over little Lago Torres in this brooding if spectacular landscape of granite and glacial retreat. The striking Central Tower was first climbed in 1963 by Chris Bonington and Don Whillans. The South Tower seen on the left is slightly higher.*

out over the strath below. Cerro Ohnet above Lago Dickson stood in the distance beside the ice-cap (it looked intriguing country) while the Rio Paine, with its glinting ox-bows, meandered towards a fine delta in blue Lago Paine below. Yes, I could appreciate how the terrain would become less and less interesting below the lake.

We must have climbed 4,000 relentless feet (1,200 metres) and the sunny morning had surrendered to a still, sullen overcast afternoon before we reached the lip of the cwm that I suspected must lie under the crest. It was an eerie place. Black rocks scattered with snow patches cradled an indigo-blue tarn. A surreal band of white quartz slashed incongruously across the black crags which reared up to a sharp pyramid-shaped summit. Two circling condors watched our every movement. Crucially, a straightforward snow slope rose to a wide col at the head of the cwm.

Reaching a pass is always exciting, especially if you're unsure if it's a pass at all. This time I was quite apprehensive as finally I crested the stony saddle. At my feet easy névé slopes swept down into a wide cwm. Below its lip the ground was

Here the rather less forbidding north-western flanks of Torres del Paine (their summits still 5,000ft/ 1,500m above us) are seen from "Campo Whillans" near the head of the Ascensio Glacier, where the valley curves round behind the Towers. The 1963 British expedition placed its Base Camp here before its ascent of the Central Tower via the notch between it and the North Tower on its left.

invisible but a glimpse of forested glen in the distance and the shape of the cloud-capped peaks beyond – the Shield was obvious – confirmed that I was standing right on the divide and it was the Ascensio Valley below.

I breathed a sigh of relief and felt not a little smug. Everyone was elated, but the wind up here was bitter and we were not down yet.

An enjoyable glissade took us swiftly to the snowline where we ate our lunch, such as it was, on a mossy bank in the lee of a large boulder while a fierce hailstorm broke around us. When it stopped we continued picking our way down the hill-side, avoiding a crag here and a snow-filled gully there. We fought through the ubiquitous zone of dwarf beech, entered the forest proper and found ourselves in the valley bottom on the banks of a fierce torrent. A few-minutes' search located a

fallen tree which I crossed gingerly, reluctant to get soaked at what must surely be the last of our difficulties. But, a short distance further on, another torrent barred the way. Wider and fiercer than the last, its milky grey-green water indicated that this was the main outflow from the Ascensio Glacier. Here there were no fallen trees. We must boulder-hop. Appropriate gymnastics led to mid-stream but the final section, wide and daunting, was best attempted without a large rucksack. With difficulty each sack was passed across before its owner made his committing leap. Mike came last. Water surging round his ankles, he balanced precariously from boulder to slippery boulder. He reached the take-off boulder when suddenly his sack fell from his back. Downstream it swept, appearing and disappearing in the tumultuous white water. Mike stood there aghast, waves breaking over his feet, clutching the broken rucksack harness.

Luckily Horacio had been scouting ahead along the river bank when he heard our shouts. Wading out into the freezing water he managed to grab the precious rucksack as it sailed by. As he checked the irreplaceable contents, Mike explained that it was only a prototype and assured us that the harness fixing system would be re-designed.

And so we came at last to Torres Base Camp, a forest glade beside the tumbling outflow stream from Lago Torres below the Towers. A couple of climbing parties were in residence, their tents supplemented by squalid lean-tos of logs and old tarpaulins, smoke drifting from every chink. Despite the reasonable weather the occupants appeared to do little except fetch water. Alastair explained to Daniel that this was what climbers term "festering" – a defeatist state of mind from which, once entered, it is difficult to escape.

We now had two days left and a mountain to climb. The route up Cerro Almirante Nieto appeared straightforward. Long slopes above the lake narrowed to a wide couloir slashing up through the cliffs to a prominent shoulder. Surely

Mike Parsons and Al Stevenson ferry rucksacks across a powerful torrent in the dense beech forest near the head of the Ascensio Valley. River-crossing is a frequent necessity in Patagonia, and, needless to say, it can be a dangerous exercise – several climbers have been drowned. A wise party treats river crossing very seriously.

Typical of the shapely outlying summits of the area is Cerro Ferrier (5,250ft/1,600m), which rises between the southern end of Lago Grey and the Ventisquero Tyndall, a major southern arm of the Patagonian Ice Cap. The picture portrays the characteristic landscape, vegetation and colours of the National Park beyond the Paine massif itself. The view is from the grounds of the Park HQ on the shore of Lago del Toro.

the snow slopes and ridge above must lead to the top? The summit I calculated was rather more than 6,000 feet (2,000 metres) above us but, fit as we were, I felt confident that an early start should see us up and down in the day.

As we plodded upwards in the dawn, the sweat trickled cold down my back beneath my lightly-filled rucksack. A familiar feeling. Often I paused to marvel at the three awesome finger-like Towers rising across the cirque. Once in the couloir however there were no such diversions and the going over awkward boulders and steep loose scree was gruelling. Fifteen hundred feet (500 metres) if it was a foot, the couloir seemed interminable and it was a great relief to scramble onto the narrow arête at its head and look down the far side over hanging ice-fields to Lago Nordenskjöld now far below. A slabby wall running with cold snow-melt guarded the shoulder and gave us two interesting pitches of roped and belayed climbing. The shoulder itself we avoided by an airy traverse high over the couloir, followed by a snow-filled gully which landed us below the steep snow slopes that must end on the summit ridge. As we kicked up the snow, I remember thinking how much I was enjoying myself and eagerly anticipated lunch on the sun-soaked summit while admiring a stupendous view. But then we emerged onto the ridge, into reality and the teeth of the gale.

"So this is Patagonia," I thought, as I felt for some good holds. "It's unpredictable but, like Robbins said, it's as stunning as anywhere in the world!"

PATAGONIA – FACTFILE

BACKGROUND

The Paine massif stands at the southern extremity of the Hielo Sur – the Southern Patagonian ice-cap which extends over 200 miles (320km) along the Andean crest, its watershed marking the Chile-Argentina frontier. This compact chain of spectacular granite spires and stupendous rock walls, the product of one-time extreme glaciation, is separated from the ice-cap by a deep forested valley, while it rises sheer on the south from rolling steppes, scattered with lakes of all sizes.

There are flowery meadows and herds of guanaco, while several small glaciers still reach the evergreen forests of Patagonian Beech. The Paine was initially explored in the 1870s and was ranched early in the 20th century for some years. It was eventually declared a national park in 1959, after climbers had just discovered the area's potential.

ACCESS

Although remote in geographical terms, access to the Paine is fairly easily via Buenos Aires and/or Santiago and the international airports at Punta Arenas or Rio Gallegos (Argentina). Onward transport is by scheduled bus or rented vehicle.

The park is efficiently run and boasts an interesting Visitor Centre. There are nominal entrance fees, but strict regulations cover camping, and climbing permits are required. Backpacking is usual and, although several basic *refugios* exist, tenting is recommended. *Arrieros* and *burros* can be hired locally to help climbers establish their base camp or to lay caches for more ambitious journeys. Supplies are available at the township of Puerto Natales 90 miles (145km) distant, but several commercial outfitters will handle logistics by arrangement.

The weather is wet, windy and unpredictable with frequent storms though little worse than typical Scottish or Norwegian weather. The best season is from December to early March.

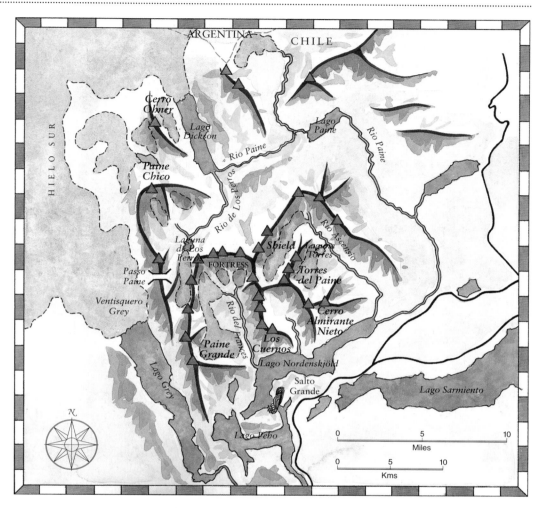

CLIMBING AND TREKKING

Although Paine Grande – the highest summit and first to be reached in 1958 – is a snow-and-ice peak, most climbers come to attempt extreme *big-wall* rock routes of up to 5,000ft (1,500m) on the massed aiguilles. No virgin summits remain but many new lines are possible.

Cerro Almirante Nieto is the only major peak readily accessible to moderate alpinists – a superb viewpoint climbed in a long day from Lago Torres. However, further mountaineering potential exists north-west of the main massif.

The map suggests many short trekking routes but the classic itinerary is the

Paine Grande	*c.10,000ft / 3,050m*
Fortress	*c.8,860ft / 2,700m*
Cerro Almirante Nieto	*c.8,760ft / 2,670m*
Torres del Paine:	
Torre Sur	*c.8,200ft / 2,500m*
Torre Central	*c.8,070ft / 2,460m*
Shield	*c.8,040ft / 2,450m*
Trident	*c.7,550ft / 2,300m*
Indian Head	*c.7,320ft / 2,230m*
Los Cuernos – Central	*c.6,890ft / 2,100m*
Cerro Ferrier	*c.5,250ft / 1,600m*

circumnavigation of the entire massif, a circuit of some seven days from the Guardaria Pehoe ranger post, a variation of which is described within this chapter.

Andes and Incas

The Peruvian Andes

MIKE BANKS

"I had seen it a hundred times on postcards but, like the Taj Mahal or the Pyramids, the real thing did not disappoint. The arresting mountain setting, the superb terraces piled one upon another, made their due impact. We sat in silence and absorbed the mountains as the Incas of old would have done."

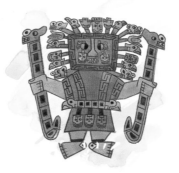

The gap was simply crying out to be filled. I was sixty and had climbed in most of the great ranges of the world. Except the Andes – the longest of them all, stretching 4,000 miles (6,400 kilometres) from equatorial Venezuela all the way down to the sub-Antarctic. I therefore blurted out "Yes!" when Mike Westmacott was only halfway through his invitation for me to join a combined trekking and climbing trip to the Peruvian Andes. I always make it a rule to say "yes" however eccentric or monstrous the proposal. Admittedly this policy may be a short cut to divorce, alcoholism or a nervous breakdown but, as they say, you should try everything once, except incest and Morris dancing. So it was that five of us flew to Lima, Peru, in August 1983 by a South American airline which allowed us an unusually generous, but very welcome, baggage allowance of 88 pounds (40 kilograms). We were badly caught out on our return flight when the allowance was unaccountably cut to 44 lb (20 kg). "Makes perfect sense," explained an old Peruvian hand. "You see, on average you get half your gear nicked in Peru! ... In Lima they can steal your socks without taking your shoes off."

Because of this predisposition of the locals to redistribute property in their favour, we had been forewarned that a do-it-yourself approach would be folly in Peru. There were stories of young trekkers being forcibly robbed of all they possessed, even down to their boots. We therefore placed ourselves in the expert hands of the premier trekking company in Peru, Explorandes, run by the charming Alfredo Ferreyros, who had been to school in England, then on to Cornell University. It was a huge comfort to know that a friendly local team would always be watching our backs.

Our small party was, if anything, a touch over-cargoed with experience and age. The first person Mike Westmacott had invited to join was his old 1953 Everest leader, John Hunt, then a very robust seventy-two, together with his charming and very fit wife, Joy. Despite his military background, John is the most unauthoritarian of men. But in his softly spoken way he is the master persuader. After a quiet chat with him you find, to your amazement, that you have volunteered for a task you would not normally have touched with a bargepole! Mike's mountaineering wife, Sally, brought with her the distinction of being the first woman to be admitted to the hitherto all-male Alpine Club of London. I recruited fellow Commando climber Rawdon Goodier (56), a zoologist and botanist. Finally there was American Bill Thomas (61), a powerful rockclimber from California who enjoyed the privilege of being able to fly first class and free to any Pan-Am destination. Once he flew from Los Angeles to London just to pick up a pair of climbing boots! He must have been very sad when Pan-Am later went out of business.

We landed in Lima under leaden skies which, combined with a generous helping of pollution, created a gloomy atmosphere, one that apparently remains from May to October and is called *Garúa*. On arrival in Lima we all enjoyed a hospitable lunch and personal briefing with the British Ambassador, Charles Wallace, an honour which, I suspect, would not have been accorded to our scruffy bunch of mountaineers had not Lord Hunt been in the party!

Next morning we escaped from Lima to fly over the Andean foothills, to look down on the russet roof tiles of the historic city of Cuzco, bathed in cool sunshine at an altitude of 10,860 feet (3,310 metres). We were immediately conscious of the reduced level of oxygen in the air. Any sudden spurt of exertion left us breathless and we knew it would take a day or so for us to acclimatise. We tried the remedy of a hot coca drink which, I suspect, gave us a cocaine-induced lift. This was followed by a glass of the local drink called *pisco sour*. Between them they did the trick.

Closer inspection of Cuzco was most rewarding. Away from the Spanish baroque of official buildings there was a maze of narrow streets and interesting alleys which invited exploration. A full day's tour around Cuzco gave us a fuller appreciation not only of the building genius of the Incas but the elaboration of their empire, which ran 1,600 miles (2,575 kilometres) from Quito in the north to Lake Titicaca in the south.

This is a characteristic image of southern Peru – peasant agriculture on the high puno, *while ice-hung mountains rise in the distance.*

101

Paved roads kept the Incas in close touch with outlying regions with a rapidity unequalled anywhere else in the world until, probably, the invention of the telegraph. Next morning we were away in an open truck to start our exploration of the Cordillera Vilcabamba which was to end at Machu Picchu. After a five-hour drive up and down valleys on precipitous roads with many a hairpin bend, we arrived at the pleasant farm of Señora Margarita Montez at Mollepata. By now we had been joined by our Liaison Officer, Pepe, complete with guitar, thankfully not amplified! I spent a lazy afternoon watching humming birds. After breakfast we drove up another 1,000 feet (305 metres) to meet our camp staff and muleteers or *arrieros*. The most important man was, of course, the cook Maxie, an amiable fellow with whom we developed the usual love-hate relationship – the lot of cooks the world over. There were half-a-dozen mules with three *arrieros*, as well as several riding horses.

We set off up a gentle valley leading towards the dominating peak of Salcantay (20,574 feet/6,270 metres), enjoying our first walk. There was a clatter of hooves as the camp staff rode by, working on the reasonable assumption that if God had meant us to walk he would not have invented the horse. Our first lunch consisted of huge and delicious avocado sandwiches. After a short afternoon walk we camped early. It is always wise to make the first day a short one.

The following day we had to cross the Incachiriasca Pass (16,150 feet/4,923 metres). Ascending to this height so early on the trek would be a real test. The pass was higher than the summit of Mont Blanc, which has been known to turn many a mountaineer's legs to lead. In the event everyone went strongly and we all arrived at the crest together. We had acclimatised well.

We descended into the next valley past the ice snout of a side glacier. When we camped our thoughts turned towards climbing our first Andean peak. Palcay had been

Nevado Alancomana (c.18,000ft/5,500m) and the Cordillera Urubamba provide an imposing backdrop to the Cuzco-Urubamba highway as it approaches the "Sacred Valley".

Nevado Veronica (19,042ft/ 5,800m), highest of the Cordillera Urubamba peaks, was first climbed by Lionel Terray's party in 1956. Here it is seen from the south over the patchworked puno *above Cuzco.*

suggested but when we saw the difficult approach and the soaring ice face we hastily lowered our ambitions. When we camped the following day it was Rawdon Goodier who suggested: "Why don't we have a go at that mountain right in front of us?" It was a rocky peak rising above a glacier and did not look too intimidating. Pepe told us that it was called Yanahumah (16,700feet/5,090 metres). Because the day was still young we decided on a quick reconnaissance of the approach.

The following morning we set off after breakfast, using a couple of mules to haul our rucksacks up to the start of the climb. There was a thin skim of crystalline snow lying on ice that was so hard that even a good jab with the boot barely gained a hold-ing for the front points of our crampons. The leader therefore seemed to be making unduly heavy weather of what looked like a very straightforward ascent. Luckily we had a number of tubular ice pitons which we used to limit the extent of any possible slip. In all there were six pitches, each of 120 feet (37 metres), which Rawdon Goodier and I shared between us. My best moment came when I had to cross a trench in the ice and climb a steep 50-foot (15-metre) wall beyond. This gave me a chance to practise the then new technique of using two short axes and only the front points of my crampons strapped on to rigid plastic boots. It worked a treat.

In due course we arrived at the top of the ice and moved towards the summit tower. Again things were not quite what they had appeared to be. In this case the rock was horribly loose. There seemed to be two breaks in the wall: a chimney with stepped ledges or a steep gully. Rawdon opted for the latter. He climbed it in crampons and I was worried to see that most of the holds were wobbly. Sometimes he seemed to depend on one crampon spike jammed on a loose hold. When it was my turn to climb I found the rotten rock really scary and was very relieved when it was over. Sally had the sense not to try. We found a small cairn at the summit, indicating that someone had been there before us. And so we stood, somewhat chastened, on our first Andean summit. What had appeared to be a pushover had turned out to be deceptively hard.

From our camp the route led downhill to join the Inca Trail running above the deep slit of the Urubamba Valley towards Machu Picchu. We now lost our sense of isolation and instead found crowded camp sites and heaps of litter. Also the trail ran along mountainsides which were too precipitous for the mules and we had to employ porters instead. Down in this sub-tropical zone our naturalist, Rawdon, found a tarantula which he cradled in his hand and offered around in case anyone felt like cuddling the hairy thing. No takers!

The fluted pyramid of Salcantay (20,574ft/ 6,270m) rises over the foothills of the Cordillera Vilcabamba in this view westward from above Cuzco.

There were three high passes ahead of us, the first and highest being Warmiw Ansuqa (13,700 feet/4,176 metres), "The Pass of the Dead Woman". It took us two days to get to Machu Picchu and, as we progressed, the number and size of the Inca ruins increased. Finally we came to a guardhouse on a ridge and beyond it Machu Picchu sprung into view. I had seen it a hundred times on postcards but, like the Taj Mahal or the Pyramids, the real thing did not disappoint. The arresting mountain setting, the superb terraces piled one upon another, made their due impact. We sat in silence and absorbed the mountains as the Incas of old would have done.

The day was advanced and we checked into the hotel to remove the grime of the journey and luxuriate in a bed. Next morning I was awake early and strolled towards the locked gates of Machu Picchu. Just ahead of me I saw a uniformed guard who, to my surprise, shinned up the fence beside the 10-foot (3-metre) gatepost and down the other side. Once he was clear I followed and found myself alone, free to roam quietly. It was enchanting. I drifted among the impeccable terraces and stairways and reflected a while at *Intiwatana*, the highest point and the sacred shrine of the Sun God.

On the Inca Trail: Mike Parsons descends the ancient steps on the strenuous short-cut that links Abra de Warmiwanusqa and Abra de Runkuraqay, the First and Second Passes.

After breakfast the gates were legally opened and I returned with the others. When the first train arrived from Cuzco and disgorged its tide of visitors we made off towards Wayna Picchu, the peak that towers 1,509 feet (460 metres) above the ruins. At first sight it looks a highly vegetated and forbidding climb but on closer acquaintance we discovered an Inca path with solid stone steps, even short tunnels through the rock, which delivered us onto the summit. We returned to Cuzco by one of those spectacular little South American railways, marvelling that it was able to cling to the precipitous cliffs of the Urubamba Valley.

A welcome hotel day in Cuzco and then we were off to the south-east to the Cordillera Vilcanota, a full day's drive through dusty, arid sierras. We dallied a while in the bustling market town of Ocongate, dazzled by the colourful hats and waistcoats of the women. We camped on the edge of the *altiplano* with the snowy massifs of Ausangate and Cayangate shimmering above the dun uplands. Our intention was to circumnavigate Ausangate (20,945 feet/6,384 metres), climbing a number of its

This is the great gorge of the Rio Urubamba, more than 2,500ft (750m) below the Inca Trail as it approaches Machu Picchu. The railway can be seen running alongside the river.

courtier peaks on the way. This landscape was very different from the enclosed valleys of the Urubamba. The open *altiplano* gave a fine feeling of space as we walked past large herds of llamas and alpacas, each with its fierce guardian dog.

Our first peak was Campa I (17,980 feet/5,480 metres), a popular and easy trekking peak above the Pachanta Pass. It gave a very curious glacier climb. For the first time we encountered *penitentes*, a name given by the Spanish to the high-pointed hats worn by penitents at Easter. In our case they were a host of small, pointed ice pinnacles eroded by the equatorial sun. It was a strange climb, slithering unroped round the tiny pinnacles, making big step-ups.

Next day I was walking alone and, as I surmounted a rise, I saw what I took to be a herd of alpacas moving across the hillside. But something did not quite fit. Suddenly I realised that they were the wild and rare *vicuña*, a smaller animal with a beautifully soft fleece which had been the sole preserve of the Inca. We also saw Andean geese, a majestically soaring condor and a marmot-like animal called *vischeccia*.

We now approached the three-headed Jatunhuma massif, modestly choosing the lowest, Jatunhuma III (19,030 feet/5,800 metres), as our next objective. It was a lumpy, glaciated mountain which would involve climbing 3,000 feet (914 metres) of convoluted glacier. The altitude would also take its toll. It was to be our highest point.

It was not a steep climb but very, very long. Much of the snow was soft, sometimes up to our knees, and there were plenty of crevasses that obliged us to rope up. The route finding was intricate, wending a circuitous trail around ice towers and through crevasse systems. At about 1PM I was in front, kicking steps, feeling the altitude and slowly counting to myself to try to keep a rhythm going. Breasting a rise, I saw to my relief that the summit dome was only a few yards away but separated from us by an ominous double crevasse. Pepe gingerly investigated the crevasse bridge and correctly pronounced it insecure. Mike Westmacott and I, who were roped together, moved left a little to try at another spot. While I made an ice-axe belay, Mike squirmed forwards on his stomach, spreading his weight as much as possible. He was midway across when there was a crunch and a lurch as the snow platform dropped about six inches (15 centimetres). Mike got the message and I have never seen a man crawl backwards so fast in my life!

We pounded rapidly downhill to find that base camp had been hit by a squall and the cook tent blown down. It was good to hear from Joy Hunt that she had climbed Campa I. We also had a change-round of camp staff: Pepe was replaced by Narciso and we were joined by a guide, Erasmo, who had been trained in Switzerland. He was a lean man who exuded quiet confidence and strength. And looks were not to prove misleading. Narciso had joined us complete with an evil-looking rawhide cattle whip. I asked him why. "Those guard dogs," he replied. "They can kill you. And they will if you go near their herd."

Our circuit of Ausangate would include crossing a series of passes which would get us into the most arresting mountain scenery of the trip. The first one took us under the lee of that elegant outlier Mariposa, "The Butterfly" (19,088feet/5,818 metres),

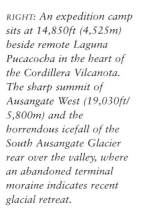

RIGHT: An expedition camp sits at 14,850ft (4,525m) beside remote Laguna Pucacocha in the heart of the Cordillera Vilcanota. The sharp summit of Ausangate West (19,030ft/ 5,800m) and the horrendous icefall of the South Ausangate Glacier rear over the valley, where an abandoned terminal moraine indicates recent glacial retreat.

and then on towards the main massif of Ausangate. Beyond the second pass we had a good close-up view of the Surimani peaks, the most dramatic of which was a towering fang of rock. We were told by Erasmo that it had not been climbed because the rock was so rotten. We therefore set our sights on Surimani Central, which would give a snow climb to a rocky summit.

We left early next morning with help from three *arrieros*. We were in three ropes: the Westmacotts; Rawdon Goodier and myself; and a Peruvian rope of Erasmo and Narciso. A long pull up a side valley brought us to the ice and the *penitentes*, through which we squirmed up unroped until we were stopped by a steep ice *schrund*. Erasmo immediately led straight up the polished and near-vertical ice of what looked like a

stone chute. The rest of us found an easier and safer route and, now roped, climbed steeply up through the *penitentes* and reached a soaring snow ridge three ropes' length below the summit. This gave elegant and exposed climbing on good snow overlying ice. The summit was a rocky perch where we could eat our lunch in comfort and marvel at the sweep of Andean landscape.

Next day we had the feeling of heading for home. In a snowstorm we crossed the Incapampa Pass and then down to the hot springs of Upis. We had a couple of days to go and I was keen to climb one last peak. Erasmo and I therefore set off with two *arrieros* to place a light camp in a valley below a snow peak called Parcocaija, which Erasmo had climbed some years previously. We camped in a high valley with our peak before us.

Next morning we were ready to go by 7AM, by which time the two *arrieros* had arrived with their mules to take our camp down. Had they not done so there was a good chance that it would have been spotted by a llama herdsman who would obligingly have removed it for us!

We circled in towards Parcocaija, which presented a steep and unforgiving face of snow and ice. The upper mountain was composed of almost vertical, layered ice. However, there was a rock band on the left which Erasmo had previously followed to more manageable climbing. The ice steepened below the rock band, so I belayed Erasmo from an ice piton while he climbed up to investigate. Using two axes and front pointing, he mounted with easy assurance. He then found that the gap had widened and there was now no way. He blamed this on the notorious warm Pacific current *El Niño*, which had caused these glaciers to retreat. He climbed gingerly down and decided to have a go at the beetling ice cliffs above us and to the right. They were nearly vertical with horizontal layering which would give a succession of intimidating ice bulges.

I drove in an ice piton for a belay. Erasmo again climbed with power and style. He moved up, across a break and then out of sight to the right and belayed. As I started to climb I found the ice was rock-hard. It took several hearty wallops before the axes would bite, which was very tiring on the arms. First up a scoop, then up left to a ledge over a small crevasse. Next a double axe pull-up over a bulge with only one dubious foothold. The ice now steepened and gave me 60 feet (18 metres) of the hardest ice climbing I had ever done. Weary with the exertion and the altitude, I arrived at the belay to be greeted by a calm and smiling Erasmo.

Erasmo then climbed another 30 feet (9 metres). The bulges presented a succession of formidable ice overhangs above him. His professional pride was, no doubt, driving him on. I saw only increasing grief and

LEFT: Johnny Fowler arrives on the summit dome of Campa I, a straightforward snow peak. Northward, across the Pachanta Pass, rise Pachanta peak (18,790ft/5,730m), on the left, and the Jatunhuma massif (20,150ft/6,140m) on the right.

BELOW: A climbing party, roped against hidden crevasses, descends the snow-covered Pachanta Glacier below Campa peak.

The Cordillera Vilcanota. A tranquil scene in the Quebrada Pucacocha shows alpacas and llamas grazing below the impressive fang of Surimani (c.17,570ft/ 5,355m). Surimani remains unclimbed, probably because of its poor rock.

suggested a retreat. Thankfully Erasmo agreed.

At the foot of the climb Erasmo suggested a traverse of the rock peak opposite us called Saglicani. A descent on the far side would then take us directly back to base camp. We climbed the rubbly slopes, skirted a small hanging glacier and arrived at the foot of an 80-foot (24-metre) chimney of horrendously loose rock leading to the summit. We climbed this very gingerly, moving from one wobbly hold to another.

We had a rest and ate some lunch on this, my last Andean summit. It had been a rare pleasure to climb with Erasmo, with his finely moulded Inca features and friendly smile. He was a born mountaineer, fluid in his movements, lean and strong.

Back at Upis we luxuriated in a soak in the stingingly hot waters and the next day strolled down the *altiplano* to the road through herds of llama and alpaca.

THE PERUVIAN ANDES – FACTFILE

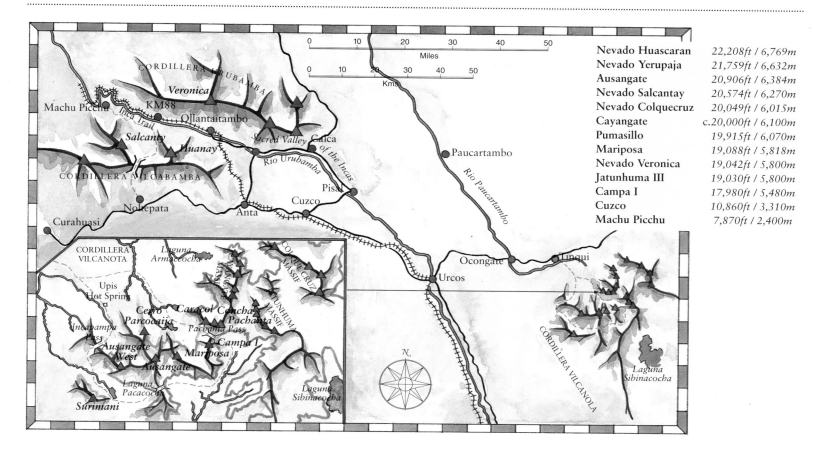

Nevado Huascaran	22,208ft / 6,769m
Nevado Yerupaja	21,759ft / 6,632m
Ausangate	20,906ft / 6,384m
Nevado Salcantay	20,574ft / 6,270m
Nevado Colquecruz	20,049ft / 6,015m
Cayangate	c.20,000ft / 6,100m
Pumasillo	19,915ft / 6,070m
Mariposa	19,088ft / 5,818m
Nevado Veronica	19,042ft / 5,800m
Jatunhuma III	19,030ft / 5,800m
Campa I	17,980ft / 5,480m
Cuzco	10,860ft / 3,310m
Machu Picchu	7,870ft / 2,400m

BACKGROUND

These are beautiful mountains, characteristically splendid ice peaks encrusted with cornices and rising above treeless golden uplands scattered with turquoise tarns where *quechua*-speaking peasants graze llamas and alpacas. Cuzco is just 900 miles (1,450km) south of the Equator so the glaciers themselves are comparatively small and typically tangled.

Although Inca tribes were no strangers to the high mountains, the history of mountaineering in Peru is recent and these southern ranges of Peru were virtually unexplored until the 1950s.

ACCESS

There are currently no access restrictions in these southern ranges of Peru and outbreaks of guerrilla activity are nowadays unlikely. As the article explains, access by road is simple from the busy city of Cuzco and approach marches thereafter are short. Nevertheless, travel is expeditionary and all supplies must be carried in. Backpacking is usual on shorter treks such as the Inca Trail, but pack animals are necessary for longer expeditions, and experienced *arrieros*, together with their *burros* and llamas, can be hired at the various roadhead villages. Alternatively, excellent local outfitters, such as Explorandes, will handle all the logistics.

The dry season here is from May to September. In theory this is winter, but temperatures can be extreme.

CLIMBING AND TREKKING

These are ideal ranges in which to climb for sheer pleasure. Although none of the worthwhile summits remain virgin, there is great scope for enjoyable, hassle-free alpine style climbing – largely on snow and ice. Even the highest peaks can be climbed in two or three days from a strategic base camp for, although proper altitude acclimatisation is essential (for both climbers and trekkers), these are not mountains of true Himalayan stature. The geography lends itself to superb trekking routes such as those described, and a composite expedition with both cultural, trekking and climbing objectives makes a most satisfying holiday. The Inca Trail itself – an ideal acclimatisation trip – is one of the world's greatest treks. Usually started from the Km 88 railway halt, it can be completed in 30 hours by a fit party, although three or four days is usual.

There are several useful guidebooks for trekkers, but for climbers prior research is recommended as no climbing guides yet exist and local maps are confusing above glacier level.

The Lonely Mountain

The Karakorum of Pakistan

KURT DIEMBERGER

"Above us soars Broad Peak. No man has ever climbed its triple-headed summit, which rises into the sky like the scaled back of a gigantic dragon. For me, the very rocks breathe mystery: nobody has touched them. I am happy that this mountain, one of the eight-thousanders, is the target of our expedition."

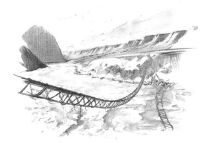

Shshsht! Shshsht! Shshsht! Shshsht! Our snowshoes glide over glistening, sunlit powder, across ribs of ice and the gently rolling curves of the glacier.

Ahead of me, still pushing strongly despite fatigue and moving with short, precise steps, is the small, almost delicate figure of Hermann Buhl, his energy clearly visible as he covers the irregular ground of the Godwin-Austen Glacier. I can see his grey, wide-brimmed felt hat above his rucksack, his fine-boned hands resting on the ski-sticks for balance each time he raises one of the oval, wooden snowshoes to take another, sliding step; but the expression in Hermann's ever-alert eyes as he scans the way ahead I can only guess at. Thus, we make our way forward, past long rows of jagged ice-shapes, as if in an enchanted forest where everything has been frozen into immobility. Corridors between the towers lead us along the spine of the moraine, through freshly fallen snow.

We are alone – alone in the heart of the Karakorum, surrounded by mighty glaciers, in a savage world of contrasts; of ice and rock, of pointed mountains, granite towers, fantasy shapes rising 3,000 feet (1,000 metres) or more into the sky, some very much more.

This spring (May 1957), besides Hermann and me and our three companions back at Base Camp, there are no other human beings on the whole of the Baltoro Glacier. Marcus Schmuck and Fritz Wintersteller from Salzburg and Captain Quader Saeed, our liaison officer (who, having no one to liaise with, has been homesick for the more colourful life of Lahore for several weeks now), are fellow members of the only expedition this season within a radius of several hundred miles. We are alone on this giant river of ice, 36 miles (58 kilometres) long, which, with its fabulous mountains, constitutes one of the remotest and most beautiful places on earth. Uncounted lateral glaciers fan out to peaks of breathtaking size and steepness – forming compositions of such harmony that they seem to emanate magic – to places where no one questions "Why?" because the answer stands so plain to see. My great ambition, to go once in my life to the Himalaya and climb the highest peaks in the world, has been realised – at the age of twenty-five. Hermann Buhl invited me to join his team on the strength of my *direttisima* climb of the "giant meringue" on the Gran Zebru (Königsspitze), a sort of natural whipped-cream roll widely considered to be the boldest ice route in the Alps to date. I'm ecstatic. Everything I have I will put into this one big chance.

Now, as we make tracks in the snow at almost 16,400 feet (5,000 metres) along one of the lateral glaciers (having set off from close to Concordia, the Baltoro's half-mile/1 kilometre-wide glacier junction), my thoughts turn to the early explorers. The glacier we are on is named after the cartographer Godwin-Austen, one of the first to set eyes on the Baltoro in the middle of the last century; but Adolf Schlagintweit was probably the first non-local to get close to the Baltoro area and to reach one – the western – of the Mustagh Passes (Panmah Pass). He has not been commemorated by name on any map. On the other hand, the beautiful, striated glacier across Concordia

from us is dedicated to the traveller G.T. Vigne, who never set foot on it. Martin Conway, leader of an expedition in 1892, was the first to come to the Karakorum to mountaineer; he was later knighted and a snow-saddle he discovered I was named after.

We are not explorers in the same sense as those men, yet on a personal level that is exactly what we are. Going into an empty landscape like this, among giant mountains, your heart quickens and the prospect around the next corner is no less seductive to you than it was to the first people who came here. The same silence dominates the peaks, the same tension arcs from mountain to mountain; days can still seem like a true gift from heaven. So it is with us on this morning ...

Above us soars Broad Peak. No man has ever climbed its triple-headed summit, which rises into the sky like the scaled back of a gigantic dragon. For me, the very rocks breathe mystery: nobody has touched them. I am happy that this mountain, one of the eight-thousanders, is the target of our expedition. But today, Hermann and I are heading off towards K2 ...

The tallest pyramid on earth seems to grow steadily before our eyes in its unbelievable symmetry. Many years ago, British cartographers computed the height as 28,251 feet (8,611 metres): 777 feet (237 metres) lower than Everest. The second highest mountain in the world is, however, considerably the more difficult of the two to climb and is,

On the Godwin-Austen Glacier approaching K2 Southern Base Camp. Broad Peak North rises opposite, right, while the glacier ahead sweeps up to the sharp Kharut peaks (c.22,000ft/6,706m) and Windy Col beyond – the Chinese frontier.

Chogolisa, known also as Bridge Peak, and her satellites are seen by moonlight from a bivouac at the junction of the Upper Baltoro and Abruzzi glaciers. In 1957 Hermann Buhl fell through a cornice on the summit ridge. He was never seen again.

without doubt, one of the most beautiful mountains in the world.

The international expedition of Oscar Eckenstein, which included the Austrians Pfannl and Wessely, made the first attempt in 1902 and managed to reach 21,410 feet (6,526 metres) on the North East Ridge. But in 1909 a large-scale expedition led by the Duke of the Abruzzi opened up the South East Spur (the Abruzzi Ridge or Rib), revealing that to be the most favourable line of ascent. They only got to 20,500 feet (6,250 metres), but on nearby Chogolisa (Bridge Peak) the Duke and his mountain guides clambered to about 24,600 feet (7,500 metres), which stood as a world altitude record for many years. They were only about 512 feet (156 metres) from the summit.

*   *   *

Hermann Buhl has stopped to look across towards Chogolisa, that shimmering trapeze of snow and ice, maybe 19 miles (30 kilometres) away. "A lovely mountain," he says. To me, it looks like aroof in the sky, fascinating beyond words, but Hermann's attention is already back with K2.

"Such a pity that has been climbed already! But wouldn't a traverse be great; up the ridge on the left, then down to the right, by the Abruzzi?" And he tells me all he knows of the Abruzzi route, how the mountain was first climbed this way by a huge Italian expedition three years ago. They achieved it with no fewer than nine high-altitude camps, and, it's said, fixed 16,400 feet

Balti porters plod up the steep trail above the Braldu Gorge en route to Askole and the Baltoro. The most dangerous section of the route, where the trail lies close to the tumultuous river and is regularly swept by stone fall, is now past and the arid valley opens slightly.

(5,000 metres) of rope on the ridge itself. Ardito Desio, a professor of geology, was leader and the two summiteers among the eleven-man team were Lino Lacedelli and Achille Compagnoni. It was a national triumph, which threw the whole of Italy into a whirl of rejoicing. It is true that they used bottled oxygen, but it ran out towards the end. And they didn't give up! Hermann is laughing, "So you see, it does work! You can do without it!" Then he tells of George Mallory and Sandy Irvine, who never came back from a summit attempt at Everest in 1924, despite taking oxygen. Nine years after their disappearance an ice-axe was found at about 27,900 feet (8,500 metres) which can only have belonged to one of them, yet today we are no nearer to knowing whether they made it to the top of the world or not. And he tells of Colonel Norton, who climbed very high on Everest without oxygen, and of Fritz Wiessner, who got within almost 650 feet (200 metres) of the top of K2 in 1939, also without using it.

I can see from his animation, from his eyes and gestures, that Hermann can hardly wait to have a go at K2, without oxygen or the help of high-altitude porters. "In West Alpine style" is the phrase he coined for it. "Mmm! K2 is a beautiful mountain and no mistake," he concludes, adding pensively, "and the way to do it is definitely up that left ridge, down the right."

But the mountain looks so high, like nothing else in the world. We are only tiny dots before this huge mass of rock, which shines like crystal from the snow and ice on its faces. It arouses no desire in me. I am happy with our choice: Broad Peak is still virgin and almost 2,000 feet (600 metres) lower than K2. Better for our "West Alpine" enterprise (which is already considered crazy by a lot of people), and better than the second-highest mountain on earth!

With that, my thoughts turn to "our" eight-thousander. The only time it was ever attempted was in 1954 by a German expedition under Dr Karl Herrligkoffer, and they found it pretty hairy. Following a line that was under constant threat from avalanches, the climbers discovered one day that huge blocks of ice had stopped only inches short of their tent. Ernst Senn, an Austrian, fell down a sheer 1,600-foot (500-metre) ice wall, whistling along like a bobsleigh to land, by incredible good fortune, safely in the soft snow of a high plateau. At about 23,000 feet (7,000 metres), icy autumn storms drained the men's last reserves of energy, forcing them at length to abandon the attempt.

A few days ago, buried in the steep ice of the "Wall", we discovered a food dump belonging to the Germans: advocaat, angostura bitters, some equipment … and a three-year-old salami, which still tasted all right. There was even a tin of tender, rolled, Italian ham, which well-travelled delicacy found its way into our stomachs. I have to confess that this side trip we're making to K2 is purely out of curiosity to see what delicious titbits might still be lying around at the site of the Italian Base Camp!

A delusion: all our efforts to find the camp fail. The wide glacier is white and pristine, and there is no trace on the moraine either. Finally, we turn around and

This is the confluence of two mighty rivers, the Biaho draining the Baltoro Glacier and, from the left, the Dumordo draining the Panmah Glacier system. Inside 3 weeks the summer melt will cover these braided flats with a roaring torrent of water, rendering river crossing a hazardous business. Outliers of the Masherbrum group are in the distance.

waddle on our snowshoes back the way we came.

It was curiosity, too, that led us to penetrate the avalanche cirque of Broad Peak. Hermann wanted to take a look at the route Herrligkoffer had chosen. The doctor had been his leader on Nanga Parbat and there was no love lost between the two men. Hermann himself had opted for a more direct line on the West Spur of Broad Peak, a line of greater difficulty, it's true, but very much safer, and one that had been recommended by the well-known "Himalayan Professor", G.O. Dyhrenfurth. A straightforward and direct ascent like this is much more in Hermann's style.

As we approach Base Camp, tired now from dragging these legs with their wooden appendages, kaleidoscopic memories dance through my mind. I remember how, amid a swirl of dust, we touched down in the old Dakota on that sandy patch of ground near Skardu which serves as an airfield; remember crossing the Indus River in a big, square boat; the three-week-long walk-in, following first the wide Shigar Valley with its blossoming apricot trees, then through the Braldu Gorge, and finally trekking up the Baltoro Glacier with our sixty-eight porters ... remember being slowed down by snowstorms, so that our loads were dumped 7 miles (12 kilometres) short of Base Camp. The subsequent load-ferrying, backwards and forwards with 55–65 pounds (25–30 kilograms) on our backs, went on day after day until Base Camp was at last established at about 16,000 feet (4,900 metres) – that is higher than the summit of Mont Blanc. And Hermann's words of consolation, "It's all good training for later on ... for the first eight-thousander to be climbed in West Alpine style."

Then the West Spur itself: up and down, up and down, plagued at first by headaches ... Later it went more easily. Whenever we set down our loads at Camp 1, we would squat on our haunches in the snow for a fast slide down into the depths again ... After a while, even taking every precaution, we could manage the 2,500–3,000 feet (800–900 metres) of descent on the seat of our pants in just half an hour – including rest stops!

Seen from Concordia, Broad Peak – this three-humped dragon – has the appearance of a mighty castle. From wherever you see it, it always looks different. You can never "know" a mountain precisely ... When we finish here, Hermann hopes to have a go at Trango Tower, or one of the other fantastic granite spires in the lower Baltoro ....

We are a modern expedition. Hermann has seen to it that we lack nothing progress has to offer. We have gas-cylinders – huge ones like those for domestic use, each a full porter-load – and small ones of about 15 pounds (7 kilograms) for higher on the mountain. We have simple, but extremely stable, ridge tents. And advanced, misshapen-looking altitude boots of heavy, solid leather. They have been made especially roomy to accommodate socks or felt

This is the "jola" bridge over the fierce Braldu River near Askole. Constructed from plaited poplar twigs, it is the traditional Karakorum bridge and is repaired only when it collapses – so say the local Baltis.

The Nameless and Great Towers of Trango, the Grand Cathedral and the Lobsang Spires are among the fabulous granite peaks that flank the lower Baltoro in this view northwards across the Glacier from Robutze camp ground.

slippers or whatever else we feel like using for insulation ... we've found newspaper works quite well! Of course, walking on moraine in these Mickey Mouse boots is awkward – you feel like deep-sea divers. No doubt one day someone will come up with a custom-made boot-within-a-boot that is a lot better. But we are not ill-satisfied. Except for one thing: progress dogs us even on the West Spur in the form of a walkie-talkie apparatus weighing 24 pounds (11 kilograms). We decide to dump it at Camp 1 (19,000 feet/5,800 metres) and from there on use the time-honoured method of a piece of paper: write down what you want to say and leave it in the tent for the others to read when they get there.

Camp 2 is a natural snow hole, which we have enlarged, under the rim of a high plateau at 21,000 feet (6,400 metres). We have even set up a kitchen there: Hermann has this weakness for potato dumplings, ox-tongue salad, mayonnaise and buckthorn juice – in other words, for all things sour – and for beer. But the latter is only available at Base Camp. He calls it Nature's Own Sleeping Draught. His first "dose" turned into a foaming fountain, 3 feet (1 metre) high, which only stopped gushing when the blue Bavarian tin was empty. Barometric pressure is quite different at 16,000 feet (4,900 metres), and we soon learn-ed to make only a tiny puncture and to keep a thumb over the

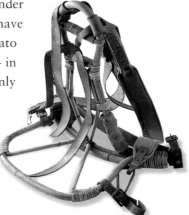

hole so that the pressure could be released slowly and our nice sleeping draught not sprayed to the four winds.

The days pass. On 29th May, we push up from Camp 3, just below 23,000 feet (7,000 metres), towards the summit ridge. We make it as far as the northern end of the "roof", that is to a height of about 26,345 feet (8,030 metres). Only then do we discover that isn't the top; the opposite end of this enormous ridge is just a bit higher. But it's too late in the day. We descend. Back in Base Camp, we know we have to retrace our steps all the way up the mountain again – just for those extra 65 feet (20 metres) of height at the other end of the ridge. There's no way round it: that is the summit!

Marcus and Hermann both have frostbite on their toes, and Hermann calls for the "doctor". That's me! Uncomfortable in the role, but using the calming words of a real doctor, I give him an injection. Then another one. Success! I was appointed expedition "doctor" only a month before our departure. Hermann justified it, saying, "Well, you've studied, haven't you?" My protestation, "Yes – but commerce," was not considered valid an excuse for refusal. He must have great trust in me. With 60 pounds (27 kilograms) of pills and potions (assembled by a real medic) and a universal tool for pulling out teeth (which by great fortune I have not been called upon to use), I'm the Medicine Man. And during the long walk-in I have been approached by many of the locals for treatment. I did what I could, relying when in doubt on my bag of painkillers. Nobody should come to any harm, at least. After all, we do have to go back the same way!

The big day – 9th June. One after the other, all four of us reach the summit of Broad Peak. Even Hermann, in the end, despite his frostbite. He had given up at about 25,900 feet (7,900 metres), but afterwards changed his mind. On my way down from the summit, I came across him still plodding upwards and turned back around to accompany him. As the day faded, this unique day, we stepped together onto the highest point ...

"It was about 7pm, the sun low in the sky, as we stood there ... Moment of truth. The silence of space surrounds and holds us. It is fulfilment. The trembling sun balances on the horizon. Down below, it is already night, over all the outstretched world. Here, only, and for us, is there still light. The Gasherbrum summits shine close by, and further away comes the shimmer off Chogolisa's heaven-

Alpenglow lingers on the north summit of Mitre Peak as night descends on Concordia 4,000ft (1,220m) below.

Gasherbrum IV, seething with mist in evening light, is seen from the west up the Baltoro Glacier. Gasherbrum VII and V stand on the right. Gasherbrum means "Shining Wall" – the name appended to GIV by Balti herdsmen who had seen its great West Face from afar, little knowing – or caring – that 3 higher Gasherbrums stood undiscovered behind it.

ly roof. Straight ahead, against the last of the light, soars the dark profile of K2. The snow around us is tinged a deep orange, the sky a pure, clear azure. When I look behind me, an enormous pyramid of darkness is thrown against the endless space of Tibet, fading with the haze into the far distance. It is the shadow of Broad Peak! A beam of light reaches out above and across the darkness towards us, striking the summit. Amazed, we look at the snow at our feet: it seems aglow. Then the light disappears ..."

(From *Summits and Secrets*, Kurt Diemberger.)

It was the great sunset for Hermann, his last on any summit.

In all truth I admired K2 from up there, that massive wedge of deep blue, like a cut-out against the flood of light. But still I felt no desire. The mountain was too big, unapproachable, easy to leave alone. No thought crossed my mind then that it was to play such a decisive role in my life. Only much later did Eric Shipton's words draw me under its spell.

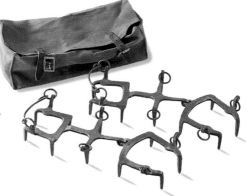

*This is K2, seen from the south at about 16,000ft
(5,000m) on the Godwin-Austen Glacier. The world's
second-highest peak, K2 is savage, unforgiving and
notorious for its sudden summit from all sides. Unlike
Everest, none of the sides are straightforward – all are
more or less dangerous. The usual route takes the
Abruzzi Spur, the steep rib furthest right, and then
follows the skyline over the prominent shoulder to
the top.*

THE KARAKORUM OF PAKISTAN – FACTFILE

BACKGROUND

The Karakorum is a trans-Himalayan range, beyond but not part of the Himalaya proper. Avenues of savage, icy peaks rear above the largest glaciers in the temperate zones – of which the Baltoro, at 35 miles (56km), is not even the longest. All six Karakorum 8,000-m peaks cluster around the Baltoro's head. Yet the deep valleys are semi-desert and only irrigation supports the sparse villages. Although once penetrated by a difficult caravan route into Central Asia, long since closed by glacier movement, the first explorers of the Baltoro were British surveyors connected with the Great Game. Younghusband crossed the Mustagh La in 1887, Martin Conway led the first climbing expedition in 1892, and subsequently the Americans Dr and Mrs Workman completed several ambitious journeys. The ubiquitous Duke of the Abruzzi made a comprehensive reconnaissance of K2 in 1909. In the 1930s Shipton and Tilman continued the exploration of the glacier and first attempts were made on K2 and Masherbrum. K2 was eventually climbed in 1954 and since the late 1970s the Baltoro has become a popular goal for both climbers and trekkers.

ACCESS

The Baltoro is currently a restricted military zone and trekking permits – which also allow climbing on sub-6,000-metre peaks – must be obtained from the Tourist Ministry.

Balti tribesman enjoy an impromptu dance below the peak of Bakhor Das (19,058ft/5,809m).

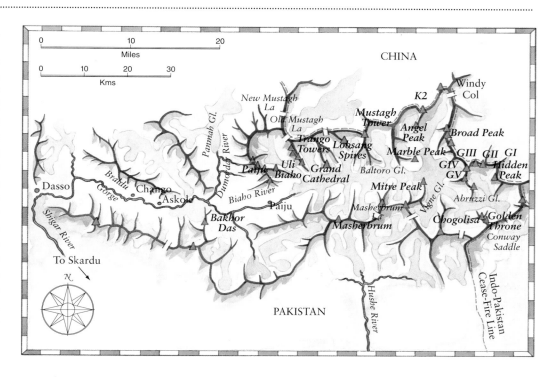

Peaks above 19,685ft (6,000m) require expensive climbing permits and a Liaison Officer. All travel to the Baltoro is expeditionary in character and it is impossible to live off the land, so all supplies must be carried in. Porters are readily available but expensive, and strict regulations govern their employment. Baltoro expeditions start from Skardu, reached by road or air from Islamabad. A road of sorts has recently been forced through the dangerous Braldu Gorge to Askole village, but it is frequently closed by landslides. Midsummer meltwater makes river crossing hazardous. May, June or September are likely to provide the best conditions for trekking or climbing smaller peaks.

CLIMBING AND TREKKING

The Karakorum is big, rugged, serious country and a trek to Concordia – a ten-day journey one way – is a worthwhile expedition in itself, especially if forays are made to Windy Col, K2 and Hidden Peak Base Camps. Challenging circuits can be made by approaching Concordia from the south via the Hushe Valley and a pass

K2	*28,251ft / 8,611m*
Hidden Peak (GI)	*26,470ft / 8,068m*
Broad Peak	*26,400ft / 8,047m*
Gasherbrum IV	*26,000ft / 7,924m*
Masherbrum	*25,660ft / 7,821m*
Chogolisa	*25,148ft / 7,665m*
Paiju Peak	*21,657ft / 6,601m*
Trango – Nameless Tower	*20,508ft / 6,251m*
Mitre Peak	*19,728ft / 6,013m*
Grand Cathedral	*19,245ft / 5,866m*
Concordia	*c.15,500ft / 4,700m*

at the head of the Vigne Glacier, or by returning to the Karakorum Highway via the Biafo and Hispar glaciers and the Snow Lake – a major journey. There is superb mountaineering of all standards around the Baltoro: K2, most serious of all 8,000-m peaks, is obviously the greatest challenge. Broad Peak is very high but comparatively straightforward; Golden Throne has been skied. *Big Wall* style rockclimbs proliferate among the Trango Towers, on the Grand Cathedral and elsewhere. The scope for new climbs at all high, medium and lower altitudes is still tremendous.

The Cow's Mouth

The Garhwal Himal of India

JIM PERRIN

"When the world was young and innocent, the Ganga rose here in Varanasi, but it retreated because of man's wickedness and retreats still. As I sit here in the stifling heat of the night, my thoughts and memories careen a thousand kilometres upriver, to the ice-caves of its present birth in the snout of the Gangotri glacier, and to the ultimate Shivalingam, the mountain of Shivling itself."

India both entrances and confuses me: the arrival by night in Delhi; the cacophonous manic jive of traffic on its main thoroughfares; the abject accepting plight of the dispossessed at every road margin; the weirdly circumlocutory process of train-booking and the frantic one of train-boarding; sticky heat and mingling odours of spice and ordure; the methodical calm of attendants handing out patched and threadbare linen sheets in the second-class sleeper; the earnest friendliness and proximity of fellow-travellers; the sear of noon-heat; the thrusting ferocity of auto-rickshaw drivers. Through all these I've just emerged into the cool peace and apartness of Shashank Singh's hotel on Assi Ghat at Varanasi, from the balcony of which at this night hour I look out across the great arc of the Ganga, mother-goddess river of all India, as it loops through the furnace plains of the north.

This is the Bhagirathi River – the infant Ganges – near Bhujbas, just more than a mile (1.6km) below its source at Gaumukh. The sharp peaks of Bhagirathi Parbat rise in the distance.

Here in Varanasi there is lightning flickering on the far bank where trees are backlit in turquoise: mynahs and the Indian jackdaws that fly open-mouthed and call incessantly are wakened by it; cicadas saw away like worn bearings; a gibbous moon climbs over the Ganga, its silvered path marked in textures of glisten and ripple. There are high scraps of cloud, vultures stretch their wings across the water, and a strange black bird plays on the hot midnight wind. Violent screaming flares up quick as brushfire amongst the riverbank poor. The devout on the Panchatirtha pilgrimage drift past, white-clad widows like wraiths heading for the clay bank to bathe, pausing by the *sati* stones that commemorate wives' burnings on their husbands' pyres, anointing the Shivalinga – the holy shafts of polished and ancient black stone found everywhere in India – with vermilion and garlanding them with marigolds.

When the world was young and innocent, the Ganga rose here in Varanasi, but it retreated because of man's wickedness and retreats still. As I sit here in the stifling heat of the night, my thoughts and memories careen a thousand kilometres upriver, to the ice-caves of its present birth in the snout of the Gangotri Glacier, and to the ultimate Shivalingam, the mountain of Shivling itself.

I remember the sustained immediacy of sensation in trekking to Gaumukh: the cold boil of the river from grimy fissures of grey ice; the *babas* and *sadhus* with whom only the most minimal dialogue was possible; the lemon Indian dawns; the way an old man under a tree ceremoniously spread his *dhoti* for his wife to sit upon; the dotterels at Bhojbasa that were surely the same birds as those I see each spring on my Welsh home hills of the Carneddau; the old woman with the Brahmin family, husband fat and self-important in front and

The temple to the Goddess Ganga Devi at Gangotri is an important place of pilgrimage. It was here, where the river plunges over impressive falls, that the Hindu saint Raja Bhagirathi chose to meditate.

her trailing nervously along the gorgeside path, a red bag balanced on her head as she sucked anxiously on the corner of her plaid shawl; the palpable devotion in which these pilgrims held the river; the sweet hay-smell of a parsley-like plant; the robin-like bird at Chirbasa with a rich dark-chestnut back and a carmine breast; meadowsweet – that filmy-fragrant summer rose of my own country of the summer stars; the faded blue Indian sky; the drifting flight of an alpine chough at 20,000 feet (6,000 metres); the inhuman scale and indifference of a world in the sculpting stage of process of creation; the crystal glitter of Shivling's great ridges above Tapoban at dawn.

It was two years ago. In Delhi the last monsoon rain beat down and moist, burnt air was like a slow, clinging slap across the face. This city breaks your heart, is first stage in a process by which you enter into the Himalayan mysteries. It's a point of disjunction, bears no relationship to your life back there. The insistent dry scrape of a

A sadhu strides up the Bhagirathi Valley trail towards the holiest place of all, the river's source at Gaumukh, some 10 miles (16km) above Gangotri.

beggar girl's thin fingers at your wrist, the gesture with her other hand towards her mouth, the lolling head of the infant whose mother, a shrivelled breast drooping from her sari, jabbers at you unceasingly outside the Mercedes showroom that "this baby will die". These are not of your own country's mindscape. You reel from them into a maelstrom where all values are whirled from your grasp. *Here* is not a place you recognise. *Here* demands of you the readiness to see things, to look at them, entirely anew.

Delhi, however much of an interlude, an annoyance, a frustration, it may seem to the unready, is the proper gateway to what the Himalayan traveller or climber must go through. Black kites circle lazily overhead; hoopoes flit eccentrically across the grass; pigs root in a dungheap; men and women shit in companionable groups below the walls of the Red Fort, then waddle duck-like to puddles to wash themselves. To fulfil the needs of India's Kafkaesque bureaucracy, I've come out to a decaying office in a tumbledown, filthy suburb. Above the official's head streamside willows wave through a broken window as he talks of water from the Ganga, the source of which he may soon issue me a permit to visit: "At holy times we put a drop of it on the tongue; we bathe in it before marriage and before death. This water has the property that it never corrupts. There are no germs in it. It is always pure. The scientists have tested it, but have not found what this property is."

In Varanasi, two years on, I remember these words as I watch the bathers in the dawn lift their brass cups to the rising sun and drink, ten yards downstream of a sewage outlet, five from a bloated corpse. Faith!

In the capital, restricted to the hotel in readiness for departure on the instant permits are granted, I watch translucent hippies waft by, nod to white-knuckled trekkers from the north of England whose eyes semaphore panic, exchange quick glances with mysterious women whose Indian adornments and languid gestures glide across white pages on which they incessantly write. Then we leave – trains, buses, the terror of a night-ride from Uttarkashi up a hundred kilometres of road with no surface, kerbed with blackness, a rage of water infinitely far beneath. Once the bus lost traction. Peering out, I saw the edge of the road crumble into the abyss. We lurched forward, somehow. But Mother Ganga's song in Gangotri soothes ...

I sit on the temple steps from which the devout bathe and listen. The high surface note is all rush and hiss, beneath it a deeper, percussive rumbling of stones and boulders pounding along the riverbed that seizes on your imagination. I feel the expansion of my own lungs, become absorbed into the rhythm of the place. Above the temple in slow, steep turns the path climbs into the Deodar woods. The deep breaths that impel you onwards are themselves an elation – that your breast could swell with so much of the living air, thin and sharp here at 10,000 feet (3,000 metres), like cold spring water after too much of civilisation's fumy wine.

I learn from those who are at home in this place. The Garhwali porters, sinewy

ABOVE: The imposing spire of Shivling – literally "Shiva's lingam" – rises at dawn above shadowed Tapoban meadow overlooking Gaumukh.

BELOW: The source of the Ganges: Gaumukh – the "Cow's Mouth" – where the Bhagirathi is born at the snout of the great Gangotri Glacier.

Overlooked by small but shapely rock peaks, the Gaumukh pilgrim trail is an enchanting trek in its own right.

and slight, trudge past as I sit drinking *chai* in the *dhaba* at Chirbasa. They walk unconcerned, 50-pound (23-kilogram) loads secured by a twist of rope, across the log over the torrent where I balanced tentatively. I watch more closely. These distant-eyed men in sacking and flip-flops move as Westerners do not move. The placing of each foot is deliberate, the transfer of weight on to it instinctive and assured. Their walking is an art that, once you have noticed, you begin to practise – too consciously and too late perhaps, and without their natural grace, but nonetheless, you have begun to learn to walk. Also, here you can begin to learn to speak, balance words, hear content and not talk merely for sound. You listen to the simplicity of porters, *sadhus*, cooks. Like that percussive rumbling deep in the river, you regain the gravity of your humanity.

For a few days, whilst the path is re-established post-monsoon and the brimming streams subside, I walk up and down to Chirbasa, stopping at the first tea-shop on the way, acclimatising, returning each evening to sleep at the tourist bungalow in Gangotri. In a damp twilight Ed Douglas and myself sit there on the terrace of the Hotel Ganga Niketan. Four Korean climbers take a table by us, appraise our gear without approval except for Ed's mountain cap, which they ask to see, examine thoroughly, ask for how many dollars he would sell it? Ed, irritated, firmly reclaims it as they list their peaks as though other items of merchandise.

To get away, I move next to a monk in saffron robes who is smoking Capstan cigarettes. Where does he live? Upriver beneath a rock in the summer; Varanasi, where he reads Sanskrit and Indian medicine at Benares Hindu University, in the winter. And his object in being here? To teach meditation and sexual healing, for which many students come to him. He makes an expansive gesture with the Capstan cigarette. I catch the eye of Sylvia, the trekker from Dresden who has joined us. She transmits a delicate scepticism. The monk is very beautiful, aware of it too in the way he caresses his long, brown hair and practises expressions on us. He looks like the young Krishnamurti, and as with Krishnamurti there is an element of mischief and showmanship about him, and just enough suspicion of charlatanry to free him from the taint of bland piety.

I visit the temple to make *puja*. The priest views my awkwardness with patient amusement. He goes to an ornate silver statue of the goddess Ganga in the dim interior to pray, returns with water in a tiny ladle which he pours into my hands to drink, and little balls of fine-ground sugar to eat, before marking my forehead first with red and then with yellow paints. Clouds drift amongst craggy spires above the village, accentuating towers, arêtes, great clefts. A lammergeyer glides across, its shadow traversing the rock face. Two helicopters fly up the gorge, minute against the peaks, their engine note absorbed into the river's roar, and we start for our base camp at Tapoban.

For the unacclimatised it's two or even three days' walk from

LEFT: The Sudershan Parbat massif rises so steeply over Gaumukh that its summits can only be seen from afar. Here the mountain is reflected in a tarn among the Gangotri moraines at the foot of Kedar Dome.

BELOW: What a pleasure it was to be greeted at Base Camp by Bham Bahadur – our loyal and brilliant cook – with his assistant and gallons of hot chai *after surviving the terrible storm on Kedar Dome.*

Gangotri, but I wonder if there's a more enchanting walk anywhere in the world? It has excitement. The path is forever changing. Rockfalls sweep down. Cliff-traversing sections – crazy wooden stemple-supported constructions – decay and fall into the glacier torrent beneath. Its population changes too. Pilgrims constantly move up and down between Gangotri and Gaumukh, as well as trekkers, mountaineers, muleteers, *sadhus* clad in the orange of renunciation, soldiers and the quiet porters of the hills. There is an intensely dramatic and changing beauty, the great gorge arcing east then south, into the sun with the high Bhagirathi peaks bright beneath it.

Beyond Bhojbasa – a tented hamlet with a mouse-ridden tin hut of a tourist bungalow – you leave behind the birch scrub and enter a province of gleaming stone newly emergent from beneath the retreating glacier, the route vague, slipping between moraines and silt-margined turquoise pools, its line marked here and there by eccentric flat-slabbed cairns, painted Hindi ideograms. Until a few years ago the path to Gaumukh and Tapoban crossed the river at Bhojbasa and held to the true left bank. Massive landslides scoured it away. Now it meanders up the right.

By the Cow's Mouth – the great fissures in the glacier snout from which the river bursts out – are more *dhabas*, their canvas shelters weighted by low stone surrounds, the proprietors squatting on sack-covered sleeping platforms within, blowing up the wood fires whose tang alerts you to their presence hundreds of yards away and setting on blackened kettles at your approach. Ash-covered *sadhus* with matted hair immerse the devout in milky water so cold it burns. The path slants beneath cliffs thousands of feet high, down which stones whine and burst like shrapnel, then debouches into the glacier. I tack inland. Glaciers! I thought they were white, gleaming places of snow and blue crevasses. This is a mile-wide highway construction site with towering hills of spoil two or three hundred feet high. House-sized blocks rumble down them; rock-slides start at a touch; voids lipped with gravelly ice, the sound of rushing water deep within, block your path. The tributary ice-streams of Chaturangi and Kirti add to the fracture and chaos. Two thousand feet (600 metres) above Gaumukh, at an altitude of 14,643 feet (4,463 metres) and after a gravelly climb that leaves you gasping for breath, you reach peace and Tapoban.

I do not know in the abstract why some places are holy and others are not, but in its human and natural detail Tapoban's distinction is palpable. You could, I suppose, question its three residents, Om Giri, Babaji and Mataji, and, though just to meet the latter – a small, dark and ageless south Indian woman – alerts you to the presence of holiness, their words won't provide any better evidence than that provided by your eyes. It's a high meadow with Shivling soaring above and strange birds, tracks of bear and snow leopard in the mud each night and herds of *bharal*. Above you, always, is the great presence of Shivling, phantasmal by moonlight, glistening in the morning sun, by turns repellent and inviting, fulfilling in its atmospheres of warm rock and furious blast, its concealments and splendours, its crystalline apartness, the notion many have that this is the world's most beautiful peak.

Twin-headed Shivling is seen in all its glory from the flanks of Kedar Dome. Rather higher than Shivling, Kedar boasts a horrific South Face, although its north-western flank is comparatively gentle and four of us tried to climb it on ski in early May. We were high on the mountain and confident that we'd cracked it when we were hit by the worst storm I have ever encountered. It came without warning and lasted, with short pauses, for 7 days. Somehow we managed to retreat unscathed.

Somehow, I do not have an overwhelming desire to reach its summit, and I have not anyhow come on this expedition as a climber. At times in Base Camp, looking up at its unworldly spire, Menlove Edwards' words steal into my head: "This climbing. Perhaps, really, one was never made for it. I have a conceit that I was even made for more than that: more than to satisfy extremely one's own pride."

It would be nice to feel that one could have possibilities of interacting in an expansive manner, contacting with life beyond and outside of ourselves. No, I do not particularly want to make things quail before me: the satisfaction of seeing them bow the head is charged too much with despondency.

All of the expedition members, I suspect, have mixed emotions towards the peak, from aching, anxious desire to the psychological devastation of abject fear. Some look wisely at the serac barrier at 20,500 feet (6,250 metres), below the final snow slope, and arrive at the detached conclusion that its threat is too great and unpredictable to put oneself beneath. Others accept the risk. There is an extraordinary degree of friction between some of the climbers, their egos and ambitions spikily conflicting, their attention on

self rather than scene. Competition and the idea of conquest dominate and are at odds with the ideals of those who visit here without those fixations.

Sylvia, who is rather wise, and I, who am a little older, gravitate together and when the time comes for her to start her further journey to Madras, I go down with her to Gangotri, out of the stone world, its rawness and the bleak attitudes engendering there. We find a room in a pilgrims' rest-house across the river from the temple. Warm water is brought to us and we wash. Hesitantly, we approach intimacy. In my poor German and her better English we explore the ellipses of communication. After the harshness of landscape and its human correlatives, there is softness and discovery. In the nights, with the rhythm of chanting and temple bells beyond the window, our bodies on the soft bed are glimmery, melding in a grace of nakedness. A space of days passes, time which feels peculiarly blessed, and then she boards the bus for Uttarkashi. I come back to a room hollowed by her leaving, collect belongings, and return in a day, fitter now, to Tapoban.

The expedition has fallen apart. I'm enlisted as a climber. Four times, by myself and with different partners, I'm drawn to Shivling's high camps and apart-world, load-carrying, feeling my way, becoming accustomed, nauseated by other

Tapoban Meadow curls round the foot of Shivling above the Gangotri Glacier. In summer it is a beautiful place, lush with alpine flowers and inhabited by 3 Hindu hermits, in winter an inhospitable white desert. Here is a trekker's camp in late May, after the winter snows but before the monsoon and the flowers. Standing back on the right is the north-eastern face of Meru, a major climbing challenge.

Seen from the South-east below Kedar Dome, Shivling appears a very different mountain. Dawn illuminates the impressive southern face – a tantalising prospect for enterprising alpinists. The East Ridge (the right-hand skyline), the Face directly below the central saddle, and the well-defined South East Ridge of the lower South West Summit have all been climbed in recent years.

expeditions' attitudes on the mountain, terrified by the sight of a Korean with cerebral oedema being dragged down, toes trailing, across the moraine of the Meru Glacier in the twilight.

One morning in particular disturbs my memory. Ed and I have spent a night of excruciating discomfort – my third sleepless one in a row – in the tiny tent at 19,000 feet (5,700 metres), and set off exhausted at daybreak up the ridge above. In the blue shadow fingers and toes have no feeling. Avalanches and rockfalls are streaming down the sunlit face of Meru across the glacier. My usual reaction to our hill rations – puking and shitting, nauseous at the grease and meat that gluttony made me force down last night – is in force. When everything has come up, the discomfort intensifies as fits of vomiting and coughing coincide to ram bile into every cavity of the head before it sprays out of mouth and nostrils to marble the snow around me green and yellow – all this to a gasping refrain of laboured breath. I'm encountering the pain of Himalayan climbing, the unfamiliar gear, the weakening resolve, the stumbling incompetence.

The rock steps on the arête ahead rear up. By effort of will I relax, determine upon rhythm and control, set to the climbing and become engrossed in its subtleties and technicality. There are two of these towers and the crux is on the second – a slim groove of red granite with festoons of fixed rope, frayed and abandoned, hanging down its sides and a ribbon of hard ice in its back. The drops to hanging glaciers on either side are immense, the risks as we solo up grave, but suddenly I'm captivated by the process of climbing, enraptured by surroundings, revelling in the certain delicacy of crampon placement on tiny flakes and fractures, the smooth lean of the body in making for ease. In a half-hour's climbing I find out for myself what fascination is in this game, and it is enough. I understand.

I watch from the lateral ridge abutting the seracs as Ed – young, fit and acclimatised – climbs the short ice-wall which is the last technical barrier before the summit. He hesitates, his feet slip in places, chips of ice shower down. I cannot see the fixed rope up which he jumars, assume he's still soloing, watch him join the three Czechs who are ahead of us, look ruefully at my single walking axe and conclude that what's ahead isn't for me.

Laurie Skreslet and Wanda Ruktiewicz hike the lateral moraine below Karcha-kund. Beyond, across the Gangotri Glacier, rear the imposing and no longer virgin western walls of Bhagirathi II (left) and III.

It's 10 o'clock on a bright, still morning, the summit 1,000 feet (300 metres) above. I go down with only a tinge of regret, knowing that I will be back now, that the lure of high places has hooked in to my resistant psyche and I'm embarked on the steepening, deadly curve by which they impart to you knowledge of their – and your – own nature.

Afterwards, by the stream through Tapoban, I rest. An avocet stalks past along the sand-flats on coppery-blue legs, upturned bill probing, pied plumage gleaming. R.D. Laing's acid illumination is my prayer to her: "I have seen the bird of paradise. She has spread her wings before me and I shall never be the same again. There is nothing to be afraid of. Nothing. The Life I am trying to grasp is the me that is trying to grasp it."

A week later, on an Agra hotel rooftop, the dome and minarets of the Taj Mahal glimmering above the haze under a bright full moon so that I ache with the evanescence of this most beautiful of human creations and finest of all monuments to human love, I have an intuition: that there are ways of approaching mountains; that properly, if your own character is to grow through contact with them, it must be by appreciation of their beauty, by respect and a desire to establish between you and your desire's object the perfection of mutual rhythm – that it must be to do with love and not the assertion of power, it must be a marriage and not a rape.

Good! Know that! Kiss the joy as it flies ...

THE GARHWAL HIMAL OF INDIA – FACTFILE

BACKGROUND

Gaumukh – the Cow's Mouth – is the snout of the Gangotri Glacier – probably the largest glacier in the Indian Himalaya – and the principal source of the holy Ganges. Known as the Bhagirathi Ganga, the river plunges over a spectacular waterfall at Gangotri some 10 miles (16km) downstream, an atmospheric place where the Hindu saint Raja Bhagirathi chose to meditate. Gangotri is now a place of pilgrimage, where the devout bathe in the infant Ganges and the fit hike onwards to Gaumukh. The first exploration of the glacier was made in 1933 by an expedition led by Marco Pallis. Shipton and Tilman arrived there in 1934 and the glacier system was properly surveyed in 1935. By 1939, several peaks had been climbed, including Bhagirathi II.

ACCESS

This is one of the more accessible Himalayan regions, thanks to military roads constructed during periods of border tension. The centre for this part of Garhwal is Uttarkashi, reached by bus or private transport in 2 days from Delhi. Porters are hired in the busy bazaar and the Nehru Institute of Mountaineering is based above the town. A mountain road continues for some 45 miles (73km) up the impressive Bhagirathi Gorge to Gangotri, whence a well-frequented pilgrim trail leads in 2 days to Gaumukh. All travel beyond is expeditionary.

Although trekking does not currently require permission, all climbing is strictly regulated: permits must be obtained 6 months in advance of arrival, peak fees must be paid and a Liaison Officer employed. Best climbing conditions are during June and September – either side of the monsoon.

LEFT: *It is spring and Hywel Lloyd slogs up the Gaumukh pilgrim trail approaching Bhujbas. The beautiful, small peak beyond, still resplendent in winter garb, also seen on p.132, is a northern outlier of Meru.*

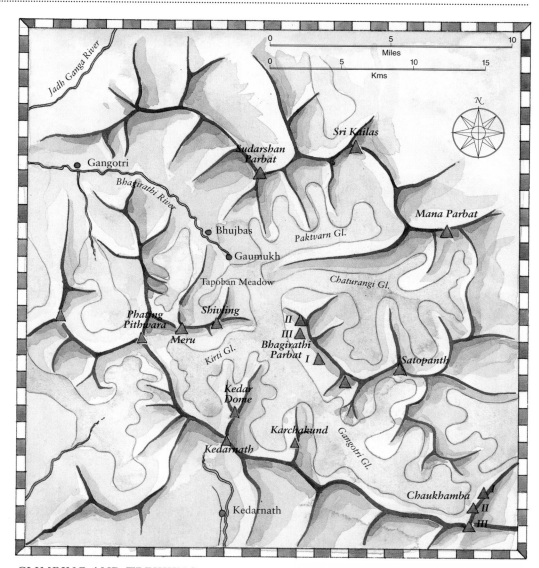

CLIMBING AND TREKKING

Once above Gaumukh there are no easy trekking circuits, although several side valleys below are worth visiting. Journeys up the Gangotri Glacier and its tributaries are rigorous but lead into most impressive scenery. The climbing on a score of fine peaks, on granite, snow and ice of all standards and at reasonable altitudes, is second to none. Shivling, Thalay Sagar and Bhagirathi III are serious mountains of world renown. Kedar Dome has been climbed and descended on ski.

Thalay Sagar	*22,651ft / 6,904m*
Bhagirathi I	*22,493ft / 6,856m*
Kedar Dome	*22,411ft / 6,831m*
Shivling	*21,467ft / 6,543m*
Bhagirathi II	*21,365ft / 6,512m*
Sudershan Parbat	*21,348ft / 6,507m*
Bhagirathi III	*21,175ft / 6,454m*
Meru	*21,161ft / 6,450m*
Tapoban Meadow	*c.14,100ft / 4,300m*
Gaumukh	*12,770ft / 3,892m*
Bhujbas	*12,440ft / 3,790m*
Gangotri	*10,000ft / 3,048m*

The Abode of the Gods

The Nepal Himalaya

KEV REYNOLDS

"Trekking in the Himalaya brings you face to face with the now of living. It teaches the value of every moment, for there's nothing to filter each new experience. These come with an immediacy that's intoxicating; one moment you're lifted by a sudden view or sound or scent; or you're faced with momentary despair as the trail plunges directly down only to rise steeply again soon after, or it's been washed away in the last monsoon or rockfall. Life is instantaneous."

Twelve days from the roadhead I came upon the first of two small glacial lakes trapped in an ablation valley below the black lateral moraines of the Yalung Glacier. Huge snow-sheathed peaks dazzled the sun and were turned upside down in the semi-frozen water, creating the kind of scene it would have been sacrilegious to ignore. So I slid the rucksack to the ground, lowered myself onto a convenient rock, and listened to the silence. I recalled reading once that silence is man's confession of his own deafness. "Whoever wrote that," I thought, "had never spent time alone in the Himalaya on a still November day."

Then I gave myself to the silence and, would you believe it, he was right. It was not silent after all. Almost devoid of sound, maybe, but not completely, for there came a hint – no more than that – of a breeze, full of frostnip scraped from that ice-face over the way. Over there, on the other side of the unseen glacier, Koktang was a crystal curtain, its immaculately fluted ridge tilting shadows to outline each individual fold and ripple. The breeze had come from the scoop of

Makalu is the world's fifth highest mountain. This is its little-known eastern flank in Tibet, seen from the high Milke Danda Ridge above the Tamur River, a superb approach to the Kangchenjunga region with the finest viewpoints in East Nepal.

the Rathong La that made a deep cleft between Koktang and Rathong, and through which mountains could be seen that belonged not to Nepal but to India. Mountains of Sikkim gave voice to the breeze. Added to that breeze came a distant tinkling sound, so impossibly whispered you had to hold your breath to make certain. It came again, then again, and was followed by a more boisterous sound as a stream broke through its late-morning glaze of ice and swirled among the pastures.

I don't know how long I enjoyed that solitude, perched upon the rock, but eventually the peace was broken by a familiar voice, followed by a cough, a hawk and a well-aimed spit as one porter after another rose over the bluff and traipsed across the yak-cropped grass, huge kitchen loads contained in wicker *dokos*, or lozenge-shaped tents squeezed with hemp and clamped to perspiring foreheads with a *namlo*, or tumpline. The juggernauts of the Himalaya were on the move again.

We didn't go far that day, just beyond the lakes to the broader pasture of Ramze a little short of the point where the valley makes a sharp curve to the north. Boktoh scratched at the sky above and behind the tents. At its feet stood a stone-walled herder's hut, a heavy padlock at its door. Our tents were pitched at around the same altitude as the summit of Mont Blanc and it was bitterly cold

Outliers of Kangchenjunga, Kabru South (far left) and pointed Rathong (left) rise on the Sikkim frontier beyond the cloud-sea that covers the Yalung Glacier. This picture was taken from the Sinelapcha La, the pass over the Ghunsa Valley.

*The properly dressed Englishman carries his rolled
umbrella even on the Yalung Glacier. Taskopkiya
(17,730 ft/5,400m) rises on the Sikkim frontier beyond.*

that night. When I braved the chill at 1.00AM for a pee all was white with frost and stars were close enough to touch. Diamonds, they were, dazzling in the velvet night so bright it was tempting to reach out, pluck them from the sky, and take them back to the tent for use as candles.

There's something about a Himalayan night sky – that exquisite blackness dusted with the nearest and sharpest of stars, and when there's a moon an ethereal glow washes mountain and valley alike with its own mystery. I remember once sitting alone on a crisp night like this on the way to Manaslu, and watching as a high corrie across the glen was turned into a cauldron of froth as a full moon rose and spilled its excesses over the corrie rim. Another night in the hidden land of Dolpo, I gazed from my hillside camp to the far end of a long valley, where a yellow moon hung below the level of my tent. I swear it, that's where it was.

Bed-tea was early that Ramze morning below Boktoh, and breakfast over before the sun. Then off in the frost-bowl, crunching round the bend of the valley towards the bulk of Kangchenjunga that formed a vast white wall at the head

Tents on the remote yak pasture of Pangpema near the head of the Kangchenjunga Glacier at almost 17,000ft (5,175m). This is Base Camp for attempts on the intimidating North West Face of Kangchenjunga itself – seen beyond.

of the Yalung Glacier. I wandered towards it through an avenue of Himalayan snowpeaks lost still in shadow. But, on the far side of Kabru Dome, Kabru and Talung, the sun, hidden still in a Sikkimese meadow, began to work its magic, until suddenly Talung alone exploded with light and ice crystals danced in the morning.

At 28,169 feet (8,586 metres) Kangchenjunga is the world's third-highest mountain, a huge massif with five major summits and as many great glaciers. In Tibetan it means "The Five Treasuries of the Great Snows", which probably refers not to its summits but to the icefields flowing from it. And like many a Himalayan giant its main summit is a sacred place, the abode of the gods. In deference to local beliefs, the first three expeditions to make successful ascents stopped just short of the crown, but as Doug Scott once wrily commented, "the Japanese, who made the fourth ascent [in 1980], trod all over the top!"

Pemba, who was with me that November morning, had been to Kangchenjunga the previous year with another Japanese expedition, and had spent forty-five days on or at the foot of the mountain. Excited to be back, he pointed

Last light catches the summit of Jannu (far left), 12,000ft (3,650m) above our camp at Khambachen kharka on the Ghunsa Khola. The lesser summits of Phole Sobithongje and Khabur stand beside Jannu.

out individual features in garbled English – the site of Camp 2, Camp 3, The Shelf – then turned to Dendi with an expressive account of every movement on that awesome face in a dialect too remote for me to decipher.

We were now on the flanking moraine with the rubble-strewn glacier just below. Ahead and to the left rose Jannu, with Khambachen beyond. A small herd of *bharal* (the "blue sheep" that are neither blue nor sheep) skittered across a gully above us and stones clattered down. I was breathless, as much with the scene ahead, above, behind, as with the altitude, and was glad of a rest when we came to a significant *chorten*, like a great milestone, erected on the crest of the moraine with Kangchenjunga as a backdrop. My Sherpa companions fell silent before this pile of rocks, from which bamboo wands wearing strips of printed cloth splayed from the top. A gust of wind snapped at the flags and disturbed the prayers. An unspoken flotilla of *Om mani padme hums* was released to the mountain deities.

On a stone slab tucked in the *chorten* Pemba and Dendi, devout Buddhists, spread their gifts of rice, flower petals carried from the foothills and small denomination rupee notes. Then in unison their prayers were mumbled in a deep chant, rosary beads flicked with broken thumb nails, the chanting now an integral part of the mountain scene. All was as it ought to be. As it had been ordained. When they'd finished, Pemba turned to me: "Now you must pray," he commanded. "Okay. What should I pray?" "You pray like we do. That you come back again."

So I did.

*   *   *

With all the major summits won, the Golden Age of Himalayan mountaineering ended decades ago. A Silver Age then began with impressive new routes being

The main trail down the valley crosses this rickety yet characteristic suspension bridge spanning the Kabeli Khola near the village of Yamphudin in the Kangchenjunga foothills. Compare this modern bridge to the picture of a more primitive counterpart in the Karakorum (see p.120).

achieved on hitherto unchallenged ridges, faces and buttresses. But now the four-teen "eight-thousanders" have become the ultimate collectables, followed closely by the highest summit on each continent.

But there are more ways to indulge a passion for mountains than scaling the highest of them all, and I for one am content now to slip away to the wild places on trails that skirt rock walls, that traverse cols below the peaks, that link valley systems and tackle glaciers rather than icefaces, and lead hour upon hour among scenes of grandeur. The lure of the wild disturbs my dreams, and the best living reality I know is to spend uncounted days and weeks wandering in the realm of the gods. Trekking in the Himalaya brings you face to face with the *now* of living. It teaches the value of every moment, for there's nothing to filter each new experience. These come with an immediacy that's intoxicating; one moment you're lifted by a sudden view or sound or scent; or you're faced with momen-tary despair as the trail plunges directly down only to rise steeply again soon after, or it's been washed away in the last monsoon or rockfall. Life is instanta-neous. All that matters are the basics of weather, demands of the trail, the next

Summits of the Singalila Danda, the crest dividing Sikkim from Nepal, rise through an evening cloud-sea. Prayer flags adorn the chorten *silhouetted on this belvedere near the Sinelapcha La, crossed by Douglas Freshfield on his ambitious 1899 circumnavigation of Kangchenjunga.*

meal and somewhere to lay your head at night. Beyond that nothing exists, while the pace you wander is perfect for absorbing the thousand and one details that create the rich mountain tapestry. Background to reality. Trekking is a means to an end and an end in itself. Years ago Bill Tilman put his finger on it when he said: "I felt I could go on like this for ever, that life had little better to offer than to march day after day in an unknown country to an unattainable goal." That's it, in a nutshell.

In the far west of Nepal, Kirken and I and a few of his boys acting as porters trekked through a Himalayan spring in country that had seen few, if any, Westerners, and were lost for days at a time. I mean truly lost, not having the foggiest notion where we were until we came upon the trails of the Humla goat people, who've been trading for hundreds, maybe thousands, of years from one side of the Himalayan Divide to the other. Flocks of sheep and goats wearing 26-pound (12-kilogram) panniers of salt or grain made dust clouds over remote passes and through mysterious valleys. We coughed our way with them, sharing the same dust and the same stars while mountains without names formed corridors to our journey.

ABOVE: I consider this prospect southwards from Point 5,255m (17,240ft), just within forbidden Mustang, to be one of the world's greatest views. Glinting in its profound gorge beneath the huge peak of Dhaulagiri, the Kali Gandaki cuts its way right through the range of the Great Himalaya.

BELOW: Tarakot gompa (or monastery), aflutter with prayer flags, stands high above the gorges of the Barbung Khola astride the entrance into remote Dolpo around the western extremity of the Dhaula Himal. We found it inhabited by just two nuns, practitioners of the mysterious pre-Buddhist Bon Rite.

In Dolpo it's mostly yaks that labour over the high passes, carrying salt from Tibet. We came across them one October descending from the Baga La (16,699 feet/5,090 metres) on the way to the turquoise splendour of the Phoksundo Lake, described so movingly by Peter Matthiessen in *The Snow Leopard*. We saw no snow leopards ourselves on that trek, but Kirken, who organises many of my remote journeys in Nepal, spent three months in Inner Dolpo some years ago with a naturalist tracking that most elusive of animals, and has an amusing repertoire of tales with which to entertain a wilderness camp. Some are even believable.

Trekking in Nepal offers a unique experience, thanks to the vision of Jimmy Roberts, a retired Gurkha officer and seasoned Himalayan mountaineer. Reflecting that much of the time spent at high altitude was pretty uncomfortable, Roberts knew that approaching the big mountains was very different. This was a relaxing experience in magnificent surroundings, with the luxury of Sherpas to cook the meals, pitch tents, break camp and look after day-to-day logistics. He reckoned that such travel would appeal to many who'd never consider themselves mountaineers, but for whom wild places held a certain attraction. He was right.

It doesn't have to be like that, of course. In the more popular regions of Annapurna, Khumbu and Langtang a series of simple lodges and teahouses make it possible to tour the valleys independent of Sherpas for weeks at a time, without humping a massive backpack. Western-style hotels they are not, but the service is adequate if you're not too particular. Mind you, plenty of novice trekkers get hung-up with all sorts of dietary and health concerns, which rather takes the

shine off being in the mountains of Nepal. On the Annapurna Circuit one year I met a tough-looking American so scared of picking up some disease from eating in the lodges that he'd taken on a local Gurung lad to carry his backpack, while he wandered the trail hugging a tin of milk powder and a pocketful of Mars Bars. Annapurna is the busiest of all Nepal's trekking regions, with Coke on offer at every teahouse, and every lodge, it seems, seducing with pizza and apple pie, rather than the standard Nepali food of *daal bhat*. But eating only Western food tends to sanitize the experience, which ought to be all-embracing and take account of the astonishing cultural diversity of the area, as well as its obvious scenic dimension. To grab the full range of wonders on offer takes effort, but it's worth it.

While trekking up the Marsyangdi towards Manang on the Annapurna Circuit, peaks were mostly shielded from view by the depths of its gorge. There were a few places where I'd glimpse Manaslu, neighbouring Himalchuli and Peak 29 (Ngadi Chuli), but crowding cliffs streaked with waterfalls soon drew the horizon into dark shadow. Then I turned a bend above Dharapani, passed through an archway *kani* at Bagarchhap, and gained a first partial view of Lamjung and Annapurna II beyond a frieze of prayer flags. This is Buddhist country, and as I progressed towards Manang and the Thorong La, the trail was punctuated with *mani* walls, *chortens* and rocks carved with the sacred rune, *Om mani padme hum*. Passing these adds merit to your journey. Often I'd study a water-driven prayer wheel, the tinkling of its bell counting off every revolution as prayers were scattered towards the Himalayan skies.

Below Manang the houses of Braga rose in tiers against an eroded cliff-face to a centuries-old *gompa* (Buddhist monastery) that contained in its musty darkness several revered Buddhas and a hundred or more terracotta images clothed in ancient dust. The toothless monk who met me there placed a ceremonial scarf round my neck and gave a blessing for my safe passage over the Thorong La. Outside, snowclouds drifted off the Annapurnas and brought an early winter, so I sat out the storm in Manang until it was safe to cross the pass and descend to Muktinath and the Kali Gandaki, the river flowing between Annapurna and Dhaulagiri through the world's deepest valley.

My own favourite valley hereabouts is the Buri Gandaki, east of the Annapurnas. It cuts a long shaft between Manaslu and the Ganesh Himal, and the trail that heads upstream from Arughat Bazaar to Samdo, the highest village, leads to enchantment everywhere. Tiny villages are perched on seemingly inaccessible ledges, a few small fields of millet ruffled by the breezes with thatched houses huddled to one side. The river has carved a series of gorges, the trail now teetering high above it, then swooping down to

We'd been away a month climbing in the Jugal Himal and on the march out we stopped at this primitive stupa outside the Sherpa village of Tarkeghyang for a group picture. Left to right: Mr Tamang, our second porter; Pemba Tshering Thami Sherpa, our cook; myself; my great chum Ian Howell; our sardar Lakpa Dorje Kumjung Sherpa; and Gayltzen Solu Sherpa, our chief porter. We'd been a good team and now it was almost over.

This khani *or chorten-arch outside the village of Bagarchhap is virtually the gateway to Manang itself, the arid trans-Himalayan valley behind the Annapurna massif. Mike Parsons checks with his map that the sharp peak that's just appeared is indeed Annapurna II – it's summit a full 19,000ft (5,800m) above us.*

post-monsoon shallows where you wade through tributary streams before clambering high above the river once more. This helter-skelter route makes no concessions to unacclimatised trekkers, and for decades bore a frightening reputation. But once you get above the village of Sho, Manaslu suddenly announces its presence. An astonishing, almost fish-tail peak, its shape changes after Lhogaon, when you climb to the former yak pasture of Syala and face an amphitheatre of mountains: Himalchuli, Ngadi Chuli, Manaslu, Manaslu North and Naike Peak. The long wall of the Kutang Himal forms a counter-balance across the Buri Gandaki. The first time I came here I'd damaged a rib in a night-long bout of coughing and spent a day in a supine position, content to just lie squinting at a vertical arctic dream. Sometimes it's good to do nothing but exist.

The easiest mountains to get to from Kathmandu are the Ganesh, Langtang and Jugal Himals, which make a long crenellated line north of the capital along the Tibetan border. There are lodges in Langtang and the nearer Helambu districts, but trekking in the more uncompromising country of Ganesh and Jugal calls for greater logistical support. Tilman led an expedition here in 1949, when he was among the very first mountaineers to gain access to what had formerly been the forbidden land of Nepal.

Unfortunately he arrived in the summer and much of the scenic wonder was lost among monsoon clouds, but he still managed to portray the glory of these mountains in the entertaining manner that was his literary trademark. A year after he'd explored the Langtang Valley, he trekked through the Khumbu to the foot of Everest, and viewed the as yet unclimbed summit from the slopes of Kala Pattar, the 18,448-foot (5,623-metre) hill above Gorak Shep. It's to Kala Pattar (a Hindi name meaning "black rock") that many trekkers puff their way each year in order to gain what has become the classic view of the world's highest mountain.

I had Kala Pattar virtually to myself after ranging for several weeks in and around the Khumbu and its feeder glens, and sat among the prayer flags attached to the summit cairn feeling small but privileged to be there. This view of Everest is a splendid one, but in some respects it's better seen from Gokyo Ri in the next valley to the south-west. From that 17,520-foot (5,340-metre) viewpoint you overlook Nepal's longest glacier, which flows from Cho Oyu, and enjoy an unforgettable 360-degree panorama that includes a whole galaxy of peaks: Everest, Lhotse, Makalu, Thamserku, Kangtega, Ama Dablam, Cho Oyu, Gyachung Kang and many more. Directly below, the turquoise jewel of Gokyo's lake contrasts the rubble-strewn glacier nearby.

*   *   *

Always looking for an excuse to return to the Himalayan kingdom of Nepal, I found myself with a contract to write a trekker's guide to Kangchenjunga and to record a radio programme for the BBC. So, inviting a group of friends, I sent a fax to Kirken in Kathmandu, and another expedition was born.

Two days' journey by bus led to Basantpur, from where our trail struck off across the Tinjure Danda in unseasonal rain. Later that first evening our camp was hit by a thunderstorm that shook the ground and filled the *charpi* with hailstones; we'd not seen a single mountain. But at 5.30AM Kirken was full of excitement: "Come see! Big view, Everest, Makalu, Lhotse Shar. Come look!" Dawn light flooded the country in the north-west, and three of the world's eight-thousanders were floating in the mists of daybreak. A half-hour after leaving camp we gained sight of our fourth, Kangchenjunga, and it seemed an arrogance to believe we'd be walking not just to the mountain, but beyond it. Another world away.

Another two camps, and we were down on the banks of the Tamur River, following in the footsteps of Joseph Dalton Hooker. The great Victorian botanist had been the first foreigner to explore these Nepalese valleys as long ago as 1848–49. Three days later we briefly left Hooker's route at Sokathum, and from an overnight camp at the confluence of the Tamur and Ghunsa Khola struggled up a steep hillside to Amjilassa. Here the valley

It rained hard most of the way up the gorges of the Buri Gandaki as we slogged in to attempt Himalchuli. It was still the tail-end of the monsoon and the river with all its tributaries was in flood. Al Stevenson sets out gingerly across a tumultuous side stream above Argat village.

of the Ghunsa Khola is narrow and very steep, and tackled on yet another day of rain made for tricky negotiation. Thereafter things improved as we moved among the middle hills, passing through Bhotiya villages whose inhabitants had crossed into Nepal generations ago from Tibet. There were yaks in the high pastures, gentians lining the trail, and the larch-clad slopes of every mountain had been brushed with the Midas touch of autumn genius. Beyond Ghunsa trees shrivelled to shrubs and shrubs disappeared as monstrous moraines cut across the valley from glens to east and west. Crossing an enormous landslide, suddenly mighty Jannu announced its presence to the right. So powerful was the vision that I was stopped in my tracks. This, the shapeliest of Kangchenjunga's satellites, had been planed smooth by the glacier below me. On the mountain bare rock topped by creamy waves of cornice shone in reflected afternoon light, and I was dazed by its beauty.

From Kambachen, highest of the valley's settlements at about 13,500 feet (4,115 metres), to the Base Camp of Pangpema north of Kangchenjunga, was a two-day trek with scenes of wonder at every step. Most of the route led along the west bank of the Kangchenjunga Glacier, sometimes in the ablation valley, sometimes on yak pastures where snow cocks chased one another with a maniacal cackling. Pangpema itself is set above converging glaciers. Around it lofty mountains carry international frontiers. Tibet to the north, India (Sikkim) to the east, while the bulk of Kangchenjunga dominates the south view. Unable to make a circuit of this huge massif since there are no permits here for cross-border trekking, we returned to Ghunsa, then crossed the Sinion La, Mirgin La and a higher, unnamed pass, each at around 15,200 feet (4,630 metres), and descended to the Simbua Khola – the valley which drains the south side of Kangchenjunga. And from there next day headed upstream towards Rathong, Koktang and the Rathong La.

Again I sat for a while overlooking the first of the glacial lakes. And listened for the silence. Then moved on slowly, for this was a homecoming that called for a reverential approach. Around the curve of the valley beyond the Ramze pastures I trod a remembered trail that led towards the southern wall of the world's third-highest mountain. And as afternoon clouds spilled over each of the five summits in turn, I recalled that morning eight years before when I'd stood there with Pemba and Dendi. Their devotions still circulated in the crisp Himalayan air as I remembered Pemba's instruction to me. "You pray like we do. That you come back again." In this abode of the gods, my prayer had been answered.

FAR LEFT: Chulu Far East is a straightforward peak of around 20,000ft (6,000m) in Manang. Seen from close below its summit, Annapurna I, trailing a snow plume, dominates the horizon. Gangapurna is the sharp top on the left while Chulu East stands nearby on the right. The climber is Shelagh Northcott.

BELOW: Mount Everest needs no introduction. It's very big, it can be quite mean and nowadays it attracts those who climb for glory. Here the summit and upper South West Face are seen from Gokyo Ri, a fine viewpoint 15 miles (24km) to the west.

THE NEPAL HIMALAYA – FACTFILE

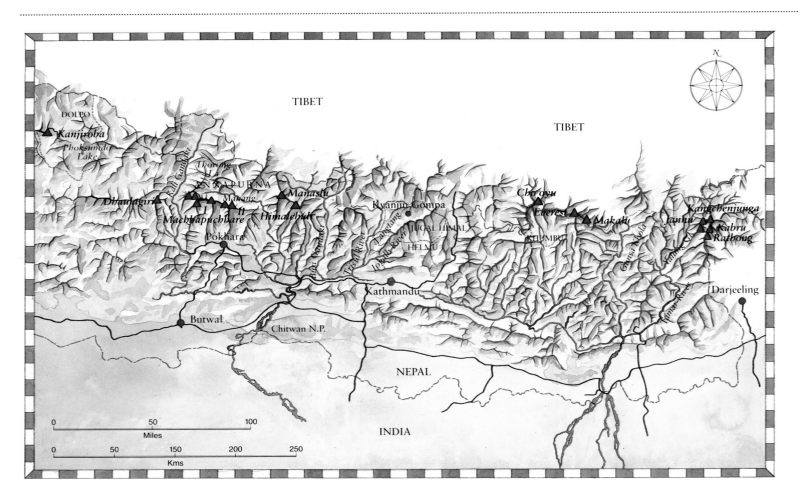

BACKGROUND

Nepal is almost entirely mountainous. Here is the greatest concentration of high mountains in the world: some 50 summits top 24,000ft (7,300m), and hundreds more rise above 20,000ft (6,000m). Ruled by the monsoon, Nepal is essentially green and fertile, a tangle of forested foothills rising gradually to eternal snows. Frequent villages scatter many of the deep valleys, which are terraced for cultivation of barley, millet and rice. Roads are rare, so that communication follows a dense network of ancient footpaths and most freight travels on man-back, occasionally on ponies and, at higher altitudes, often on yaks. Nepal was designed for walking and its people are typically proud, smiling and hospitable, although

often they are also desperately poor. The Gurkhas and Sherpas, known for their loyalty, are but two of the ethnically diverse hill tribes. After Nepal opened in 1948 all exploration and climbing involved long treks of necessity. "Trekking" as we know it was invented in the early 1960s when Jimmy Roberts, a retired Gurkha officer, realised that the trek was a marketable holiday. Trekking and climbing are big business in modern Nepal.

ACCESS

Approach is usually via Kathmandu international airport and Trekking Permits for the area to be visited must be obtained before leaving the city. The Climbing Permit system is complex, expensive, demands a Liaison Officer

Mount Everest	29,028ft / 8,848m
Kangchenjunga	28,169ft / 8,586m
Lhotse	27,940ft / 8,516m
Makalu	27,766ft / 8,463m
Cho Oyu	26,906ft / 8,201m
Dhaulagiri I	26,795ft / 8,167m
Manaslu	26,781ft / 8,163m
Annapurna I	26,545ft / 8,091m
Annapurna II	26,040ft / 7,937m
Himalchuli	25,896ft / 7,893m
Jannu	25,292ft / 7,709m
Ganesh I	24,298ft / 7,406m
Kabru	24,124ft / 7,353m
Ama Dablam	22,494ft / 6,856m
Rathong	21,909ft / 6,678m
Boktoh	20,151ft / 6,142m
Thorong La	17,771ft / 5,417m

and must be organised months in advance. Several border areas and many fine peaks remain off-limits. However, certain so-called Trekking Peaks may be attempted on an extempore permit with minimum formality and cost. Buses and regular STOL flights facilitate travel east and west from Kathmandu. It is often possible to backpack and live – very simply – off the land, particularly on popular trekking routes, where tea-houses have proliferated. But travel elsewhere is expeditionary, several porters will be necessary, preferably with a *sardar* (mandatory when climbing) to organise them and a cook to pamper you.

CLIMBING AND TREKKING

For climbers the several hundred Permitted Peaks (none of which remain virgin) offer plenty of new routes. Siege tactics, oxygen and big expeditions are, these days, considered inappropriate, and ideally climbs should be attempted in alpine style. The current 18 Trekking Peaks – the highest standing at 21,600ft (6,584m) and several of them really challenging – offer good value to recreational mountaineers. Trekking routes range from short, easy valley hikes, via popular circuits, such as that to Everest Base Camp or around Annapurna, to serious journeys in remote and unfrequented country, crossing glacier passes where mountaineering skills are essential for safety and survival. The logistics of any trip should be organised through one of the many trekking outfitters in Kathmandu such as Col Roberts' firm, Mountain Travel. Climbers and trekkers alike should treat altitude (say 16,000ft/4,800m and over) very seriously. AMS (Acute Mountain Sickness) regularly kills and there is no substitute for proper acclimatisation.

An expedition porter at work high above the gorges of the Ghunsa Khola on the Kangchenjunga approach march. All transport and commerce in the mountain country depends on such sturdy fellows, real experts in their gruelling profession.

Snow on the Equator

East Africa

H. W. TILMAN

"On Kenya is to be found climbing at its best. There is no easy route up
it, but much virtue may be got from a mountain without climbing it.
For those who are not compelled to answer its challenge, let them camp
near the solitudes of its glaciers, to gaze upon the fair face of the
mountain in sunshine and shadow, to watch the ghostly mists
writhing among the crags and pinnacles, and to draw strength
from her ruggedness, repose from her aloofness."

POINT PIGGOTT

Piggott is a peak that is nearly all ridge, a continuation, in fact, of our west ridge, but cut off from the main peak by the col from which we began our climb. The real summit of Piggott lies at the north-east end of the ridge and thus overlooks our col, but it was too steep to tackle from there. We gained the summit ridge further to the east after some difficult climbing, and the summit itself was not reached until 1PM. The mists were late in forming that morning, so that we were rewarded with glorious views of the west ridge and face, together with a great expanse of territory below us. The dark green of the forest merged into the wide grey-green sea of the plains, a vague, shadowy surface streaked with the darker lines of bush growing by the watercourses. This was bounded on the north by the Loldaika Hills, beyond which the green changed to brown, and the brown to yellow, as the arid sandy wastes which stretch to the Abyssinian Highlands took possession. To the south, cloud hid all but the loftiest of the Aberdares, allowing us no glimpse of the snows of Kilimanjaro, 200 miles (300 kilometres) away, which once or twice have been seen from high up on Kenya.

Our descent was enlivened by a variation which at first promised well, but later involved us in a long rappel; and on the way to camp we passed the skeleton of a buffalo at about 15,000 feet (4,500 metres). We got home in a snowstorm at five o'clock, pretty tired.

In the night there were ten degrees of frost. We lay long in bed and had an easy day looking for a tarn which, from the top of Piggott, had attracted us by its brilliant, emerald-green colour.

On the 8th we made a grand circular tour of the peak, passing to the west of Piggott, and by Two Tarn Col to the Lewis Glacier, which we crossed to get home again by four. Near Point Lenana we found a thermometer dropped by S.'s [Shipton's] party in 1929; the height was about 16,000 feet (4,800 metres) and the minimum reading was thirteen degrees – nineteen degrees of frost. The extreme cold which we had felt, after our return from the traverse of the peak, even inside the hut, made us doubt the accuracy of this reading. We left a thermometer of our own in the same place to be collected later. The ponies were to come up for us on the 10th, so the 9th was devoted to the climbing of what we called Midget Peak, a very pointed and precipitous little rock needle on the south side of the mountain, which only lack of time had prevented us having a go at on the previous day. We fully expected the climbing of it would afford some amusement, nor were we disappointed.

Mount Kenya, its glinting snows an unexpected sight on the Equator, is seen from the north-west near Timau, at a distance of about 16 miles (25km). The peaks visible left to right are Sendeyo and Tereri, Point Lenana, Nelion and Batian (the twin summits), and Point Piggott. It is easy to appreciate how the central peaks are all that is left of the core of a primeval volcano.

We reached it by the same route at 9.30AM, and started climbing by a gully in which there was rather more snow and verglas on the rocks than we liked. Higher up the difficulties increased, progress became slow, and snow began falling steadily. I suppose we should have turned back, but mist hid the summit and we expected every pitch would prove to be the last. S. led over several critical steps, one of which, a sloping ice-ledge, I had later particular reason to remember.

A great block crowning the summit was reached soon after one o'clock. Mist hid everything, the snow fell more heavily, and we immediately began the descent, feeling some concern at the condition of the rocks, rendered doubly difficult now by the fresh snow. Crossing the sloping ledge with more haste than caution, the new snow came away and I with it. What happened then I do not know, for my next recollection is standing on a rock platform holding a disjointed conversation with S., who was now about 80 feet (25 metres) above me. My first question was true to form, because on the stage, when the heroine recovers from her faint, she usually gasps out, "Where am I?" before once more relapsing in to semi-consciousness and the arms of her beloved. With me it was no idle question, because I had a very strong impression that we were on Kilimanjaro, an illusion only dispelled by repeated assurances to the contrary from S. Physically I seemed to be all right, but mentally I was all wrong – perhaps the jerk of the rope had knocked me senseless. Nor were my mental anxieties any less when I found that this descent of mine by a new and very quick route was of no use, because I had reached an impasse and had to climb back to join S., assisted by the rope.

ABOVE LEFT: Climbers on the shore of Harris Tarn begin the ascent of Point Lenana by its North East Face.

CENTRE: Tereri and Sendeyo rise beyond Kami Hut on the shore of Kami Tarn.

ABOVE RIGHT: Batian and Point John (right) loom over Hut Tarn after an overnight snowfall in August.

A second attempt to traverse the iced-up ledge was successful, and the descent continued over rocks which seemed to become colder and more difficult every minute. Wherever it was possible, we roped down on a doubled rope, making eight or nine in all of these rappels. Had the descent continued much further we should have run out of rope, because we had to cut 18 inches (46 centimetres) or more off each time to make a rope ring through which to pass the climbing-rope. We were singularly ill equipped for this travesty of climbing, necessary though it was since we had with us not even a pocket-knife, so that the rope had to be hacked through with a sharp stone.

However, we got down, still with some rope in hand, collected the ice-axe and rucksack which we had left at the foot, and trudged heavily up the Lewis Glacier for the third time, in soft new snow. (This glacier, by the way, was named after a Professor Lewis, an American geologist who accomplished some revolutionary work in the study of glaciers.) It was not altogether a surprising thing that I now began to feel as though in the course of the day I had come into violent contact with some-

Point John casts its sharp shadow on the snows of Point Lenana – seen at sunset from the summit of Nelion.

The abseil from Batian into the Gate of the Mists – the icy notch between it and Nelion, the lower of the twin summits.

thing hard; in addition, both of us were very wet, and neither of us was strong-minded enough to deviate from our route to collect the thermometer left near Point Lenana. It was probably buried deep under snow anyway, and no doubt it still lies there, taking temperatures which no one will ever read.

On the 10th we did nothing but lament the fact that the ponies would not arrive until evening, for we now realised that we had very little food left to see us down. Three came up, and on the 11th we made a double march to our first camp at the edge of the forest, which was reached at five o'clock in rain. We had nothing left to eat but a small quantity of one of those food beverages which are a household word. Perhaps we had insufficient, but we began to suspect that the claims made for it were as hollow as our stomachs. This camp in the forest, which should have been doubly pleasant to our senses, starved by many days lived amongst rock and snow, was for us merely an irksome delay before the satisfying of our more animal wants.

We were horribly weak as we crawled feebly down next day to the farm from which we started. Bacon and eggs there at 10.30AM, and lunch and beer at noon, were partial restoratives, after which we settled our accounts, and left for home.

This was, I think, the most satisfying fortnight either of us ever spent or is ever likely to spend in Africa. On Kenya is to be found climbing at its best. There is no easy route up it, but much virtue may be got from a mountain without climbing it. For those who are not compelled to answer its challenge, let them camp near the solitudes of its glaciers, to gaze upon the fair face of the mountain in sunshine and shadow, to watch the ghostly mists writing among the crags and pinnacles, and to draw strength from her ruggedness, repose from her aloofness.

Few are the countries that, having no traditions, have in their stead such a symbol and an inspiration.

The lush crown of a giant groundsel (Senecio keniodendron) – the characteristic plant of the Afro-Alpine zone – beside little Oblong Tarn contrasts with craggy Point Peter rising over Hausburg Col (left). "Window Ridge", a grade VI rockclimb, follows Point Peter's left skyline, taking its name from the conspicuous hole.

RUWENZORI

We camped in a damp but welcome cave at about 13,000 feet (3,900 metres), hard by the Bujuku Lake, a mournful, shallow mere which, with its fetid, mud-lined shores, was in harmony with the desolate landscape surrounding it. But from the cave our eyes lingered, not on this, but on the grim precipices across the valley below the snows of Mount Baker, on the serrated ridge of the Scott-Elliott Pass, and the peaks and glaciers of Mount Stanley. This, however, was a view which was seldom, if ever, seen in whole except for a minute or so at dawn or dusk, so that we were usually compelled to trust to fleeting glimpses of rock and ice, peak and ridge, seen through the writhing mists, and in imagination link the whole together.

Our first plan had been to carry all our own food and kit to an advance base near the Scott-Elliott Pass – a pass lying between Mount Stanley and Mount Baker which we hoped would give us access to both mountains. It was some time before the mist cleared sufficiently for us to identify the pass, and from that distance it looked as though the approach to it might prove too much for our porters. We had already sent eight of these down, retaining six with us in the cave. They were comfortable enough and moderately content, but were so daunted by the appearance of things higher up that it seemed advisable to leave them out of our calculations and shift for ourselves. On account, therefore, of this alteration in our plans the afternoon of our arrival at the cave was a busy one, sorting out food and kit for ourselves for five days, and making it up into two loads of 40 pounds (18 kilograms). We intended to establish our camp on the Stanley Plateau, from there climb Margherita and Alexandra, move our bivouac nearer to Mount Baker and climb that before returning to the cave to refit. We had yet to discover that as the hare must first be caught, so, on Ruwenzori, the peak must first be found.

We left camp at eight on the morning of the 17th, with two men carrying our loads. Skirting the lakeshore, we climbed through senecios, reached the rocks, and at about 15,000 feet (4,500 metres) came upon the site of a former bivouac. It was now eleven o'clock, and, as snow was beginning to fall, we sent the men back to the cave, shouldered our 40-pound packs, and climbed slowly upwards. About one o'clock we reached the foot of the Elena Glacier, and, climbing now on snow at an easy angle, we presently reached the yet flatter slopes of the Stanley Plateau. The weather was thick, so that our sole guides were infrequent glimpses of the rocks of the Elena and Moebius Peaks close on our left. By three o'clock we were completely at a loss as to our whereabouts, so we pitched our little tent

ABOVE: A Bakonjo porter scurries over the Scott-Elliot Pass (14,350ft/4,374m) below the unclimbed 1,300-foot (400-m) West Face of Semper – a thoroughly forbidding wall, and probably the major outstanding problem in the Ruwenzori.

LEFT: The roof of the Ruwenzori: this is the view south-eastwards from the summit of Albert to Margherita – the highest top – with Alexandra beyond. The scale is deceptive for Alexandra is only a quarter of a mile (400m) distant.

ABOVE: *Dawn behind Mount Baker is seen from Mount Stanley's Elena Glacier. Left to right, the summits are Monk's Head, Semper and Edward – the highest.*

RIGHT: *Two climbers on the South East Ridge approach the rime-encrusted summit of Alexandra. This is the regular route and presents little technical difficulty, although the best way of reaching it depends upon the state of the cornices and crevasses.*

in what we imagined was a sheltered spot, and prayed for the mist to lift. At sunset the longed-for clearing came, showing, to our amazement, our camp pitched almost on the divide. A few hurried steps up a snow-slope, and we were brought to a stand as much by a view which held us spellbound as by the sudden falling away of the ground at our feet. Far to the west and below us, through a rift in the driving clouds, we could see the dark green, almost black, carpet of the Congo Forest, upon whose sombre background was traced a silvery design by the winding Semliki River. To the south showed a lighter patch, where the waters of Lake Edward reflected the last light of day; but in a moment sinking sun and rising mist merged all but the snow at our feet in a once more impenetrable gloom. Of more practical value to us than this wonderful sight was the exposure for a brief minute of a snow ridge to the north leading up to a peak which we knew must be Alexandra. In spite of the conditions, we had pitched camp in a position well placed for an attempt on this peak, and we turned in with unjustified complacence, for it was more by good luck than good management. It snowed all night and was still snowing at dawn, so that the clearing from which we had hoped to refresh our memories never came. When we started at 7.30 to try to "hit off" the ridge which we had seen the previous evening, visibility was limited to about 10 yards (9 metres), and, after wandering perplexedly for two hours amongst a maze of crevasses, we returned to camp. Caution was needed, as tracks were obliterated by fresh snow almost as soon as they were made.

The persistent snow soon found the weak spots in our little tent, which was not well adapted either for sheltering two men or for use on snow. Pools of water soon accumulated on the floor, limiting the area at our disposal, an area already made small by an inconvenient centre pole, so that it became increasingly difficult to keep our sleeping-bags dry. In the evening another clearing in the mist caused us to dash out, but we only got as far as the foot of the ridge before gathering darkness compelled us to return.

On the third day it was still misty but the snow had stopped falling. Assisted by our tracks of the previous night, which in places were still visible, we reached the ridge and began climbing. Except for one awkward cornice and the uncertain quality of the snow, the climb was not difficult, the summit (16,703 feet/5,091 metres) being reached by midday. There was a patch of rock on top where we found a cairn in which were records left by the Duke of the Abruzzi in 1906 and Dr Humphreys in 1926. We sat there till 2.30PM, but caught only passing glimpses of the neighbouring summit of Margherita. Camp was reached at 4PM, when a brief clearing enabled us to wring out our sleeping-bags and bale the tent. Our success on Alexandra, combined at sunset with another remarkable view of the Congo and a sight of the Margherita Ridge, sent us to bed in a more or less contented frame of mind.

More snow fell in the night, but we turned out at 7.30AM and were rewarded by seeing Margherita clearly for five minutes. By the time we had got under way, the mist had re-gathered, so that in a short time our ideas as to position and direction became as nebulous and woolly as the mist itself. The crevasses seemed more numerous and the mist thicker than on our first attempt, but, after groping about for some hours, we saw looming before us what was undoubtedly a ridge. At the foot of it was a steep rock buttress, which we managed to turn on the right,

John Temple in action on the scrambly, lichen-hung South West Ridge of Johnston, the third summit of Mount Speke. The southern peaks of Mount Stanley rise across the Bujuku Valley with Elizabeth on the left (above the hanging Coronation Glacier), Savoia in the centre, and Elena on the right.

traversing back above it to the left. Hopes ran high as we reached the crest of the ridge and began to follow it, but next moment we stood dumbfounded, staring, Crusoe-like, at footprints in the snow. Such was our bewilderment that wild and impossible conjectures of another party on the mountain flashed across our minds before we realised the unflattering truth that these were our tracks of the previous day, and that we were climbing Alexandra for the second time.

We crept back to camp with our tails well down, to pass a rather miserable night, depressed as much by our failure as by the state of the tent, whose contents, including our sleeping-bags, were now sopping wet. Our food was almost finished, but before our forced descent on the morrow we determined to have a final crack at Margherita.

By three in the morning we were so cold in our wet sleeping-bags that we gave up trying to sleep, brewed some tea, and prayed for dawn. Camp was struck, the sodden loads packed, and at six we moved off down the glacier, dumping the loads near the foot of the Stanley Plateau. Then, in a last

This is the beautiful little summit of Kitasamba, an outlying pinnacle of Savoia and a portal of the Coronation Glacier on Mount Stanley.

desperate resolve to find the Margherita Ridge, we turned north again. The usual mist prevailed, while the width and frequency of unbridged crevasses made vain any attempt at following a compass course, which in any case could only have been an approximation.

These repeated changes of direction enforced on us by the crevasse tried our tempers severely; every change gave rise to heated argument, during which each of us would fall to drawing little maps in the snow with ice-axes to illustrate our respective theories.

Once more a rock buttress loomed up. It was viewed with suspicion and tackled without enthusiasm, while every moment we expected to come once again upon our old tracks. In this we were delighted to be disappointed, and at eleven o'clock we reached the summit of an undoubted peak, but which we could not tell. It was snow-covered, so there could be no records to find; all to be done was to wait for the mist to clear. This we did, sitting in a hollow scraped in the snow.

We descended the couloir below the narrow Savoia-Great Tooth Col, and the first abseil dropped over a huge cornice into this eerie ice-cave. Below, steep ice and snow slopes took us down to the Elena Glacier.

The climb had been an interesting one but not difficult. The ridge and the summit were draped with cornices of a strangely beautiful feathery appearance. Very little melting appears to take place at these heights, so it is possible that this formation is due to wind rather than rapid alterations in temperature. On the other hand, the presence of numbers of large ice stalactites under the cornices suggests a considerable range of temperature.

Unless another night without food was to be spent on the glacier, our departure had to be timed for 3PM. A searching wind began to lessen our interest as to what peak we were on, threatening to drive us off its summit with our knowledge unsatisfied. Time after time the swirling mists seemed to be thinning. Repeatedly we would take off our snow-glasses in the hope of finding a tangible clue in the sea of fog, only to be baulked by fresh clouds rolling up from some apparently inexhaustible supply. Repeatedly we were disappointed, but at last a clearing came. It lasted hardly a minute, but it was long enough for us to see and recognise the familiar summit of Alexandra, and to realise from its relative position that we must be on Margherita (16,763 feet/5,109 metres).

It was sheer luck to have hit off the ridge on such a day, so that we were almost jubilant as we started down. Helped by our outgoing tracks, we reached our rucksacks at 4.30PM, and, stopping only to swallow a mouthful of raw pemmican, we hit out for the cave. In spite of mist and gathering gloom we found the route, quitted the snow for the rocks, slid and slithered down mossgrown slabs, and soon were fighting our way through the senecios above the lake. Burdened as we were with water-logged packs and exhausted by our previous efforts, our condition was such that our progress was governed more by the impulse of gravity than by our legs. So with one mind we steered straight for the mud of the lakeshore, knowing that it would be soft, but doubting whether a quicksand itself could be worse than the senecio toils in which we were struggling.

It was not a quicksand, but a very fair imitation, and withal, very evil-smelling; "Here, therefore, they wallowed for a time, being very grievously bedaubed with dirt; and Christian, because of the burden that was on his back, began to sink into the mire." Frying-pan and fire, devil and deep sea, Scylla and Charybdis, all seemed weak comparisons for the horns of our dilemma. Finally we took once more to the senecio forest – perhaps because it did not smell – and by nightfall reached the cave and welcome warmth of a roaring fire.

EAST AFRICA – FACTFILE

BACKGROUND

Mount Kenya is the eroded plug of an ancient volcano standing in isolated splendour 10 miles (16km) south of the Equator. Rising abruptly from a dome of high moorland and surrounded by clustered aiguilles, the twin summits are hung with 15 tiny and fast-shrinking glaciers. Unknown to Europeans until 1849, Batian was first climbed by Mackinder and two Courmayeur guides in 1899; Nelion, 30 years later by Shipton and Wyn Harris.

The Ruwenzori – a *block mountain* – is by contrast a range of several large massifs surrounded by heavily forested foothills extending 70 miles (110km) along the Uganda/Congo frontier. The six highest hold small glaciers and ten of their many summits top 16,000ft (4,800m). Mentioned by Ptolemy, these legendary "Mountains of the Moon" were hardly explored until the Duke of the Abruzzi's Italian expedition made the first ascents in 1906.

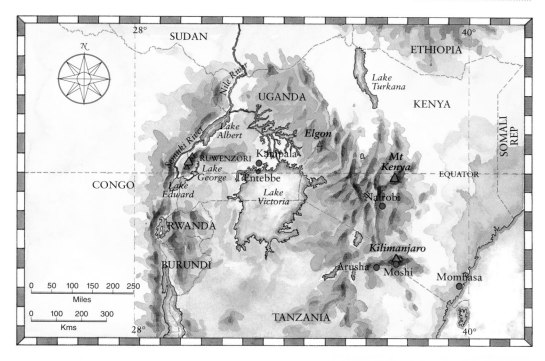

ACCESS

All access to Mount Kenya National Park is regulated, and entrance and overnight/camping fees are charged. Bona fide alpinists pay less than trekkers, who may hire guides and porters. The nine strategically located climbing huts are small and currently decrepit. There are also several convenient caves. On three of the seven main trails that approach from the encircling main road, it is possible to drive to 10,000ft (3,050m). On the mountain's southern flank, January and February give summer conditions while winter occurs in August and September. The opposite is true for the northern flank. Between these periods are the Rains.

Ruwenzori access is expeditionary and approach from Uganda is recommended for political and practical reasons. Ibanda is reached by bus and taxi from Kampala. Here permits are obtained and porters hired, but there are strict rules for their employment and equipment. Seven strategic huts are currently ruined but caves are plentiful and tents are recommended. The weather is typically awful but is at its best in January, February and July.

CLIMBING AND TREKKING

Mount Kenya offers dozens of excellent alpine-style climbs on rock, snow and ice that are comparable to those on the Chamonix Aiguilles. The easiest route to the main summits of Batian and Nelion is a serious IV inf., essentially a two-day climb. Proper acclimatisation to the height is essential.

With its tarn-jewelled cwms and linking passes, the surrounding moorland offers superb trekking with ascents to such straightforward tops as Point Lenana.

A fit party can reach the heart of the Ruwenzori within three hard days. Thus a ten-day circuit via Kitandara and the two main valleys, crossing the Scott-Elliot and Freshfield Passes, makes a fine, if rigorous trek through the incredible *afro-alpine* vegetation for which the Ruwenzori is renowned. The main summits are rewarding and provide fairly straightforward single-day snowclimbs from the higher bivouac huts. However, predictably horrible weather and vegetatious rock blunt everybody's desire to attempt difficult climbs.

Mount Kenya:	
Batian	*17,058ft / 5,199m*
Nelion	*17,022ft / 5,188m*
Point Lenana	*16,355ft / 4,985m*
Point Piggott	*16,265ft / 4,957m*
Point John	*16,020ft / 4,883m*
Tilman Peak	*c.15,700ft / 4,785m*
Point Peter	*15,605ft / 4,757m*
Tereri	*15,466ft / 4,714m*
Sendeyo	*15,433ft / 4,704m*
Midget Peak	*15,420ft / 4,700m*
Ruwenzori	
Mount Stanley:	
Margherita	*16,763ft / 5,109m*
Alexandra	*16,703ft / 5,091m*
Albert	*16,690ft / 5,087m*
Savoia	*16,330ft / 4,977m*
Moebius	*16,134ft / 4,918m*
Kitasamba	*c.15,950ft / 4,862m*
Mount Speke:	
Johnston	*15,860ft / 4,834m*
Mount Baker:	
Edward	*15,889ft / 4,843m*
Semper	*15,730ft / 4,795m*

INDEX

Caption information for chapter openers
p.10 *Below the Brèche de Roland on the northern French side.*
p.22 *A camp on the Eiger West flank with the Jungfrau beyond.*
p.40 *First snow on the "Five Sisters of Kintall".*
p.56 *View over Kinney Lake towards Whitehorn Mountain.*
p.70 *Climbers on the summit Feather of Eagle Tail Peak.*
p.84 *Ventisquero de los Perros pours off the Paine Grande massif.*
p.98 *Llama at the head of Quebrada Upismayo, below Ausangate's NE face.*
p.112 *Balti expedition porters on the Baltoro Trail.*
p.126 *Bhagirathi II and III rise beyond the moraines around Gaumukh.*
p.142 *Above Camp II on the NE Ridge of Himalchuli.*
p.160 *A view over Nelion's southern flank from Batian.*

ACKNOWLEDGMENTS

The publishers would like to thank the authors, trustees and publishing houses of the following publications and articles for their kind permission to reproduce their text in Distant Mountains.

"Mohammed's Bridge" Nicholas Crane,
an extract from *Clear Waters Rising* (Viking, London, 1996) and reproduced with the kind permission of A.P. Watt Ltd on behalf of Nicholas Crane, and Penguin Books Ltd, London. Text copyright © Nicholas Crane, 1996.

"The Roof of the Alps" W.M. Conway,
extracts from "Mont Blanc" and "Bernese Oberland" published in *The Alps from End to End* (Archibald Constable & Co., London, 1905).

"The Undiscovered Country" W.H. Murray.
First extract from "The Undiscovered Country" published in *Undiscovered Scotland* (Dent, London, 1951). Second extract from "Twenty-four hours on the Cuillin" published in *Mountaineering in Scotland* (Dent, London, 1947). Text copyright © Anne Murray, 1947 and 1951.

"The Light of Other Days" David Harris.
Text copyright © David Harris, 1998.

"The Land of Red Rocks" Steve Roper.
Text copyright © Steve Roper, 1998.

"The Unpredictable Mountain" John Cleare.
Text copyright © John Cleare, 1998.

"Andes and Incas" Mike Banks.
Text copyright © Mike Banks, 1998.

"The Lonely Mountain" Kurt Diemberger,
an extract from "The Lonely Mountain" published in *The Endless Knot* (translated from the original German by Audrey Salkeld; Grafton Books, London, 1991). Text copyright © Kurt Diemberger, 1989.

"The Cow's Mouth" Jim Perrin.
Text copyright © Jim Perrin, 1998.

"The Abode of the Gods" Kev Reynolds.
Text copyright © Kev Reynolds, 1998.

"Snow on the Equator" H.W. Tilman,
an extract from *Snow on the Equator* (G. Bell and Co., London, 1937). Text copyright © Pamela H. Davis, 1993.

The publishers owe thanks to the following organizations for the loan of equipment for studio photography.

Cotswold Essential Outdoor
For all your outdoor equipment needs
P.O. Box 75
Cirencester
Gloucestershire GL7 5YR
Tel: 01285 643434

Lowe Alpine
Clothing and Equipment.

in the UK
Lowe Alpine (UK)
Ann Street
Kendal
Cumbria LA9 6AA
Tel: 01539 740840

in the USA
Lowe Alpine Systems Inc.
2325 West Midway Boulevard
P.O. Box 1449
Broomfiled
Colorado
CO 80020
Tel: 303-465-3706

in Canada
Daymen Outdoor Marketing
100 Spy Court
Markham
Ontario L3R 5H6
Tel: 416-298-9644

p.89 photo credit
Ultra Quasar by Terra Nova Equipment Ltd.
PHOTO: Terra Nova Equipment Ltd.

Duncan Baird Publishers and John Cleare would also like to extend special thanks to the library staff and Committee Members of the Alpine Club, London, for their enormous help with research for this project, and their kind loan of Victorian Alpine equipment for studio photography.